Energizing
the Congregation

Energizing the Congregation

Images That Shape Your Church's Ministry

Carl S. Dudley
and
Sally A. Johnson

Westminster/John Knox Press
Louisville, Kentucky

Scripture quotations from the New Revised Standard Version of the Bible are copyright © 1989 by the Division of Christian Education of the National Council of the Churches of Christ in the U.S.A., and are used by permission.

Lines on page 40 from "Lead On, O Cloud of Presence," a hymn text by Ruth Duck, are copyright © 1974 and published in *Everflowing Streams: Songs for Worship* (New York: Pilgrim Press, 1981).

The chart on pp. 110–111 from Carl S. Dudley, Jackson W. Carroll, and James P. Wind, eds., *Carriers of Faith: Lessons from Congregational Studies* (Louisville, Ky.: Westminster/John Knox Press, 1991), is reprinted by permission of the publisher.

Book design by Patrick Bobbitt

First edition

Published by Westminster/John Knox Press
Louisville, Kentucky

This book is printed on acid-free recycled paper that meets the American National Standards Institute Z39.48 standard. ∞

PRINTED IN THE UNITED STATES OF AMERICA
9 8 7 6 5 4 3 2 1

Library of Congress Cataloging-in-Publication Data

Dudley, Carl S., 1932–
    Energizing the congregation : images that shape your church's ministry / Carl S. Dudley and Sally A. Johnson. — 1st ed.
        p.   cm.
    Includes bibliographical references.
    ISBN 0-664-25359-8 (pbk. : alk. paper)

    1. Church renewal—Case studies.   2. Identification (Religion)—Case studies. I. Johnson, Sally A., 1947– . II. Title.
BV600.2.D74 1993
250—dc20   92-29814

For Carl's parents, Harold and Margaret,
*who believed that weaving faith and history
can shape the future.*

And for dj,
*who raised Sally to love the church
as she loved it.*

Contents

Introduction

This book celebrates congregations in their communities—a wide variety of real churches in real communities. Through six cases, or character studies, of particular congregations we profile five integrative self-images that church leaders can use to mobilize members in active ministry. Our focus is particularly on community outreach ministries, but the images can be used to interpret other aspects of the congregation's life and work as well.

As the cases will show, these self-images cut across lines of denomination and theology, social status and community location, size and resources. They are not limited by such circumstances, because they are rooted more deeply in each congregation's own sense of what it is and always has been.

Embedded in the language of church members and implicit in their behavior, self-images represent the core values and commitments by which they reaffirm and live out their sense of belonging. Leaders will find these self-images more in the congregation's shared memory than in its theological statements, more in its life-style than in its publicity. Images are not precise definitions, but symbols around which congregations gather for ministry. They are not the boundaries at the edges, but the banners at the center.

For the past decade the Center for Church and Community Ministries has worked closely with church leaders to strengthen congregations while developing their community ministries.[1] These various local programs reflect our own faith commitment that, by divine call and social reality, healthy congregations will be renewed in reaching out to their communities. This book is built on that commitment.

Through the generous support of the Lilly Endowment, we have had a rare opportunity to work with a wide variety of congregations, from

evangelicals to moderates to liberals. In all, we have worked with more
than one hundred Midwestern churches representing eighteen denominations, in congregations from crowded inner-city streets to affluent
neighborhoods to small rural towns. The cases we have chosen for this
book represent that variety. Denominationally they include Christian
Church (Disciples of Christ), Evangelical Lutheran Church in America,
Evangelical Covenant Church, United Methodist Church, and United
Church of Christ. Contextually they represent inner- and outer-city
neighborhoods, medium-sized communities, and a small rural town.

We first arrived at these particular five images early in 1988,
through reading narratives written by members of about forty congregations. Asked to explore their own history and heritage with respect to
their church's relationship to its community, they told individual stories that clustered into patterns. We read, studied, and analyzed their
narratives through a variety of frameworks—and then brought our
intuitive impressions to bear as well. Through all our disciplined analyses, some churches simply sounded like pillars in their communities;
others told stories of pilgrimage; still others spoke a fierce and proud
language of survival.

After identifying the five major patterns through stories, we tested
them in two ways. First, we compared them with the results of several key questions from a congregational survey that all participating
congregations had taken in September of 1987. We found significant
correspondence between our narrative patterns and the responses
congregations gave to certain questions about ministry. The results of
that study are reported in the chart "Churches by Self-Image" on
pp. 110–111.

And second, we talked with the pastors and lay leaders and with
others who had observed these churches over time—Church and
Community staff and denominational leaders. Without first telling
our identifications for each church, we described the images and
invited people's responses. In most cases they confirmed our own
hunches. Where they did not, we took a second look and renegotiat-
ed our understanding of the congregation.

While both of us have shared in shaping this material from the
beginning, and both contributed significantly to the content of all eight
chapters, in preparing the manuscript Carl took primary responsibility

for drafting chapters 1, 2, 5, and 8, and Sally was the primary drafter of chapters 3, 4, 6, and 7.

In the four years since we began developing the images, we have explored their implications with a variety of groups—in workshops, leadership retreats, long-range planning committees, and seminary classes. Everywhere we have gone, we have seen people become excited as they recognized their own church among the images and suddenly understood it better—and more hopefully—than they had before. We have heard pastors and lay leaders claim their images and talk about them long afterward as they work out the implications for their life and ministry together. If even a small portion of their excitement shines through in this book, if other congregations can catch similar visions and find new life and energy, then our purpose will be satisfied.

Among the many people who have contributed immeasurably to the development of the images and this book, we must first thank the congregations that are profiled here, both in the major cases and in the added examples. To these congregations and their pastors and lay leaders who have spent time with us and shared so candidly their own reflections, we are deeply grateful. This is their story. We have used the actual names of the churches and towns, but have given pseudonyms to individuals in order to protect their privacy.

Several members of the staff of the Center have been helpful to us throughout this project; in particular, William Boerman-Cornell, Susan Sporte, and Thomas Van Eck have contributed their comments and insights, and we thank them. Our editor at Westminster/John Knox, Alexa Smith, believed in our book from the beginning and has given invaluable advice along the way.

Finally, we offer our gratitude to the following pastors and teachers: Philip Amerson, William Burton, Richard Carlson, Mollie Clements, Jean Erb, Hugh Halverstadt, Richard Hull, Dan Lybarger, Carl McKenzie, Lincoln Richardson, David Roozen, Patricia Tucker Spier, Timothy Sporrong, and Robert Susman. We thank them not only for critiquing our work, but for pushing us to think more carefully and articulate more clearly, for what they have taught us about leadership through their own work, and for their friendship and encouragement along the way.

CARL S. DUDLEY

SALLY A. JOHNSON

1 Introducing Congregational Self-Images

Congregational unity, direction, and energy often seem unattainable in this era of mobile populations and declining institutions. Churches try to incorporate members who bring widely different denominational and cultural backgrounds, lifelong residents and newcomers who are only passing through, old-timers who may want more stability and younger members just beginning their families. Add to the picture the blur of a pastor who has only recently arrived and will typically depart within five or six years—and we wonder why churches are declining!

But congregations represent more than the aggregate faith of assembled individuals. Congregations carry a corporate character that is developed in response to their experience in ministry. In claiming that identity, even churches in a mobile society can attract, sustain, and inspire members to live out their faith together.

To mobilize churches, members rally around the language and symbols of their values-in-action, the styles of ministry that inspire their members to make sustained commitments. Those images of ministry must be clear enough for newcomers to understand them, strong enough to support people who need help, and challenging enough to enable the community to grow together. One pivotal element of identity is a congregational self-image that provides coherence to the members and direction for their activities.

IMAGES AS A SOURCE OF UNITY

From the beginning, the church has found unity and purpose in powerful images. Jesus was more a storyteller than a systematic theologian. "Jesus told the crowds all these things in parables; without a parable he told them nothing" (Matt. 13:34). He used commonplace images, often with a unique twist, to embody the mysteries of God's love in unforgettable stories, events, and characters: the good Samaritan, the rich fool, the lost coin, the Pharisee and the publican, the two sons, the two debtors—each is a classic because it describes the way things are and challenges believers to confirm their faith in action.[1]

From this wealth of possibilities in the Bible, church leaders find particular images that give coherence and direction to the congregation as a whole. When the apostle Paul was confronted with factional conflict among Corinthian Christians, he both described their problem and inspired their unity by offering them an unforgettable image: "Now you are the body of Christ and individually members of it" (1 Cor. 12:27). This image of individual members incorporated into the continuing body of Christ has served to consolidate diversity and inspire ministry through the centuries.

For church leaders, images offer three related functions: they describe, predict, and inspire the congregation.[2] As description, images must build on commonly agreed perceptions and experiences. Paul, for example, after reference to Christ's sacramental body in 1 Corinthians 11, challenges the Corinthians by comparing their disruptive behavior at the meal with their common commitment to Jesus Christ. Despite the diversity of their gifts and functions, members in Christ are made one by the spirit of the risen Lord.

Moving from description to prediction, Paul says, "If one member suffers, all suffer together with it; if one member is honored, all rejoice together with it" (1 Cor. 12:26). Almost in the same breath, Paul offers the inspirational consequence of being members in one body by reciting the familiar "Hymn to Love": "And I will show you a still more excellent way. If I speak in the tongues of mortals and of angels, but do not have love, I am a noisy gong or a clanging cymbal" (1 Cor. 12:31–13:1). The body of Christ, by accurately responding to the need of a particular situation, has confirmed commitments and released energy among believers.

CONTEMPORARY IMAGES

The five images central to this book emerged as we listened to congregations tell stories about their efforts to reach and relate to the communities in which they live. Congregations have in common a commitment to Jesus Christ. Yet as we listened we heard that churches experience that faith with different perspectives and pass it on with different emphases. In the flow of their stories we find basic patterns emerging. From the experiences they tell, we focus their story-patterns into five lively, contemporary images.[3]

The power of compelling images depends for us, as it did for Paul, on the believer's foundational commitment to the experience of God in Christ. With that faith firmly in place, we explore the ways congregations highlight some elements and diminish others. In seeking images that mobilize these churches, we are guided by several considerations. As with Paul's reference to the body of Christ, we look for images that describe, predict, and inspire the church.

Though all the biblical metaphors are possible candidates, we are attracted to fresh images that are grounded in contemporary metaphors and experiences. Yet totally novel images will not serve. Rather, we look for contemporary images that also have clear connections with the historic and biblical witness of the church.

We look for images that unite like flags rather than divide like fences. Images, raised at the center of congregational life, are less precise than concepts that define and specify. Images can arise from several different values, and therefore may overlap one another without conflict.

We also look for language that incorporates both the content of faith and the style of ministry. Images should reflect members' convictions, feelings, and rhythms of ministry, without being wed to particular language. We hope congregations will try on these images to see how they fit, with full and frequent tailoring to match in particular situations.

Finally, we look for images that the parish recognizes and claims. As we have shared these five images, congregational leaders have responded with the delight of recognition and the satisfaction of shared experiences.

As we survey their stories, we find that some congregations anchor their images in particular places or specific populations; we call them

Pillars and Pilgrims. Some congregations emphasize conditions of crisis in their ministries, some barely persisting and others aggressively proclaiming—the Survivors and the Prophets. Some congregations modestly seek to care for others—the Servants. These five images reflect the different stories that churches tell of their adventures in relating their faith to their communities.

MINISTRIES TO PLACES AND PEOPLES

A sense of responsibility is one dominant theme in the ways congregations tell of their efforts to relate to the people of their communities. Some congregations embrace the whole area, assuming a comprehensive accountability for the spiritual and physical well-being of people who live and work there. We call this a Pillar church.

The *Pillar church* is anchored in its geographic community, for which it feels uniquely responsible.[4] The architecture often reflects this self-image: the strong pillars that lift the roof physically reflect a membership that lifts the community spiritually. In a small town the church building may be modest, though it will be more imposing in a neighborhood where prominent architecture is appropriate. Like the building, the members are pillars of the community, good citizens individually and corporately. More than the building, they share a Pillar mind-set. They are ready to use their resources of facilities, finance, leadership, and heritage to strengthen the whole community.

The stories of other churches reflect a sense of responsibility not for the whole area, but for a particular segment of the population. Their caring community is not limited to a particular geography; rather, they draw members primarily from a specific cultural, racial, ethnic, or national group. We employ the image of the Pilgrim as the church that walks with its people. Some congregations are so steeped in Pilgrim theology that they can absorb other sojourners in their common pilgrimage.

The *Pilgrim church* dwells with its own people wherever they are, sustaining them as a community in their pilgrimage.[5] Their culture and their Christian faith are woven into a single fabric of church life. Some Pilgrim congregations have moved with their people from one dwelling place to another. With a strong pilgrim theology some churches embrace waves of immigration or racial change, as an established Swedish church may assist an immigrant Asian congregation, or old Slovaks may embrace young Mexicans. They live a theology of pilgrimage that reaches out to help others who travel a similar journey.

For both sorts of churches a sense of caring responsibility dominates their histories. The Pillar church cares about the place, the whole community, for which it feels accountable to God. The Pilgrim church provides the focus of faith and culture for a particular people.

MINISTRIES IN CRISES:
REACTIVE AND PROACTIVE

Some churches relate their histories as responses to crises. These congregations are more conscious of the drama of life and exhibit higher levels of commitment in response to crises they face. Some churches tell stories of living from one crisis to the next, often barely surviving on the edge of oblivion. But for these congregations, outliving disaster is not a new adventure. We discover they have been barely surviving for many years. We call them Survivor churches.

The *Survivor church* loves to tell stories of the storms it has weathered.[6] Often the congregation attracts and sustains people who take pride in their survival time and again. Survivor churches live on the edge, always on the verge of being overwhelmed by emergencies. They do not expect to conquer their problems, but they will not give in. They are determined rather than domineering, relentless rather than aggressive. They hang on long after others would have quit, because "we've made it through worse than this before." Although outsiders may see these churches as weak, they can be resilient, productive, and loving when leaders learn to make good use of their crises.

In another pattern of church stories, crisis is important in a very different way. These congregations are sharply critical of the evil, corruption, and sin they find in corporate institutions and public behavior in their communities. They often initiate action to change what they perceive as destructive and unjust. In the tradition of the Old Testament, we call these Prophet churches.

The *Prophet church* attracts members who feel called to challenge the evils of the world—from communities to corporations, from individuals to national governments.[7] Independent, often entrepreneurial in style, Prophet churches—or prophetic segments in a larger church—draw strong support from members who share their commitments. Because of their high profile, they are often used as a standard against which other churches measure their social commitment. Prophet churches share with Survivors a sense of crisis that demands high levels of commitment. Whether large or small, they often have a significant impact on community consciousness in areas of their concerns.

Although both the Survivor and the Prophet build on the energy of crises, they are very different in appeal and performance. Survivor churches are reactive, always responding to crises that come upon them, barely able to keep up. Prophet churches are proactive, converting particular situations into campaigns to challenge and transform some larger evil in the world.

FOR JESUS' SAKE, THE SERVANT

The most universal theme is found in stories of caring for persons who need assistance. All churches tell service stories, each in its own style. The Pillar church organizes programs for service, and the Pilgrim specializes in responding to the needs of its own people. The Survivor accepts each new crisis as yet another problem, and the Prophet turns personal needs into public issues. But one pattern of stories from another kind of church recalls how the congregation responded as needed to each distinctive individual. We call these churches Servant churches.

The *Servant church* attracts people who like to help others in modest ways of quiet faithfulness.[8] They visit the sick, take meals to the bereaved, and send cards to the shut-ins. Beginning with their own members, it is a natural extension to provide food, clothing, and other basic needs to their neighbors. Servants see individuals in need and reach out to help them in supportive and pastoral ministries. They live their faith in simple service.

In summary, then, the images reflect the ways congregations respond to human need: The *Pillar* church has a sense of civic responsibility that embraces the community. The *Pilgrim* church cares for the cultural group as extended family. The *Survivor* church reacts to crises in an overwhelming world. The *Prophet* church is proactive to translate crises into causes. The *Servant* church reaches out to support individuals who need help.

MULTIPLE SELF-IMAGES

Some congregations fit easily within one self-image, but most churches have elements of several. The pastor or lay leaders may hold a different image than the members at large hold. Age groups or other segments of the congregation may see the church through different lenses. The dominant self-image of the congregation may have changed over the years.

One church, for example, is seen as a Survivor by denominational staff who have debated closing it for years, yet the members see themselves as moving from Pilgrim to Prophet as community conditions change. Another church is proud to be an innovative Prophet in its community, yet it is seen as a Pillar in its activist denomination—an Old First Church and progenitor of many churches. We know of one congregation that carries all five: with its impressive architecture and a downtown location it looks like a Pillar, but the ethnic unity of the members feels like a Pilgrim; it now faces declining resources that lead to Survivorlike speeches, and a younger group of leaders are divided between Servant programs and prophetic campaigns.

At the same time, these five congregational images span the denominational and theological spectra. From our experience, the images appear with about equal frequency among all churches—although Pillar occurs slightly more often, and Prophet somewhat less frequently as a congregation and more often as a segment within a larger fellowship. Catholic and Protestant evangelicals, moderates, and liberals are well represented throughout the types. Although social location and membership size are influential, neither determines the congregational image, as we shall discuss in the case studies that follow.

Self-images are not always positive. Some are negative, and some are even destructive. Since congregations carry multiple images, church leaders can emphasize positive aspects and ignore or even challenge negative dimensions. We offer these five images as descriptions of the way churches are, as predictions of the style and content of their programs, and as sources of inspiration to gather new commitments for the ministries that members want to do together.

USES OF IMAGES

Because these images are embedded below the surface in the fiber of congregational consciousness, they function like a gyroscope to sustain the direction in which the congregation is moving. When they are recognized and discussed, church leaders can reaffirm their commitments or intentionally set a new course for congregational ministries. Recognizing these images serves several important functions.

First, by claiming the appropriate style leaders can invite and inspire a congregation to live up to its best. The church is no longer oppressed by alien expectations, and leaders now have self-selected criteria that can challenge members to do ministry in their own way, and do it well. From the resources of the Pillar to the tenacity of the Survivor, each image has its own strengths to be developed in ministry.

Second, by naming the appropriate images leaders can shape programs and organization accordingly. Leadership styles, board patterns, program choices, and partner selections are all related more to congregational self-image than to polity or theology alone. Pilgrim churches, for example, will always "keep it in the family."

Third, leaders who recognize the variety of self-images can use diversity in positive ways, constructively channeling differences among individuals and between congregations. By recognizing different congregational self-images, church leaders can affirm those that seem positive and deny or challenge those that are negative. Congregations can change directions, and members can change commitments.

Further, congregational images allow members to appreciate basic differences between congregations. All five approaches can invigorate the faith of congregations, and all five can empower churches to reach out into their communities. But they do it differently, each with its own style, its own unique mixture of commitments. By recognizing appropriate styles of ministry, churches can claim their own story, acknowledge their need for others, and strengthen the interdependence of churches working toward a common end while contributing differently.

NEXT STEPS

Images are disembodied ideals unless they live in the activities of particular congregations. In presenting these five images, we offer case studies from congregations that embody the essence of each. Since these cases reflect the idiosyncrasies of real life congregations, the ideal image will not fit perfectly. In each we explore the ways they carry out their ministry, as a particular congregation and as a representative of that viewpoint. In discussion we offer additional examples to suggest the diversity within a common theme.

The final chapters offer guidelines for leaders in applying these five images. In chapter 7 we discuss the implications so that leaders may utilize—and at times even transform—the congregational images they find. In chapter 8 we suggest possible applications in congregational development, first within a particular congregation, especially in worship and spiritual development, evangelism, and stewardship, and then beyond the congregation in community-wide strategies for refreshed awareness, new resources, and stronger coalitions for community outreach.

2 The Pillar Church:
The Story of West Street
Christian Church

P illar churches offer the entire community a source of strength, stability, and religious vision. From the solid architecture to the most recent members, West Street Christian Church provides an excellent example of a congregation that labors to serve at the center of its community life. With a comfortable bond of competent lay and professional leaders, church programs reflect a Christian concern far beyond their own members. When their partnership in ministry is threatened, the church provides stability in the storm, absorbing some damage while reaffirming basic community values.

THE HEARTLAND

"Heartland" is what the natives call this prairie of luscious, flat, black soil, where the patchwork fields alternate between heavy crop yields of basic grains and livestock quietly grazing. Farm homes are set back from the highway among other buildings, protected by summer shade trees and a windrow of evergreens. Along the highway new homes offer shelter for industrial and commercial wage earners who want the open sky but are no longer needed to till the soil—symbolizing basic changes in once secure relationships on these rich lands. Many of the houses stand alone, reflecting the oft-spoken hope of their owners that "we can make it on our own."

From this horizontal landscape of almost limitless humus, the town of Tipton rises as an island of relatively tall structures. The town offers the reassuring profile of a county courthouse and business oasis for this farming region.

At the beginning of the twentieth century, the crossing of two railroad lines, from north to south and east to west, sparked the rapid and solid growth of Tipton. Grain elevators and local banks supported expansion, farming and business supplies were available, and a variety of commercial ventures prospered. On the west side the old families of wealth constructed large homes with the gracious lines of Greek Revival designs, while on the east side a robust blue-collar community grew up around the Catholic church and school. By the mid-twentieth century, state highway construction linked the town and county with surrounding cities, attracting several substantial industries to diversify the local economy.

The last two decades, however, have been hard on Tipton. The town was hit with a disastrous downturn in farm income, the development of a shopping mall that drained business from the center of town, the outside purchase and relocation of major local industries, the controversial consolidation of the school system, and, most recently, the lost autonomy of local banks that were integrated into the regional financial systems of distant metropolitan areas. One after another, these blows reduced the town's self-sufficiency and deprived citizens of access to once-assured resources. Almost half of the residents now commute to nearby cities to find jobs. As it was from the beginning, the enduring wealth for the area resides in the growing power of the land.

WEST STREET CHRISTIAN CHURCH

Along with grain elevators and municipal buildings, the spires of several church steeples can be seen from a distance, reaching above the trees and homes of the community. Three old Protestant churches are within two blocks of the center of town. Although slightly different in design, they were all built of the same solid rock construction during the first decade of this century—when the railroads puffed energy into Tipton.

Of the dozen-plus Protestant churches throughout the town, West Street Christian Church has the largest membership and the most active program. Church members quietly recall the church's founding by Dr. Silas Blount, who preached the gospel in his log cabin in the early 1840s, even before the early settlers drained the swamp and claimed the land for farming. The Methodist and Presbyterian churches also claim a spiritual legacy from Dr. Blount, but not so early or with such assurance.

The exterior of the West Street Church building is attractive in a muscular way, with lines designed to emphasize more its strength than its beauty. Inside, brown and burgundy carpets guide the visitor into a sanctuary that reflects a more feminine design, with vaulted arches, off-white walls, and stained-glass windows, one of Jesus with Mary and Martha, and one with the woman at the well, etched in deep, primary tones of green, red, and especially blue.

In one corner is a soundproof nursery, with cribs for babies and toys for small children; on the other side, a coatroom with a small assortment of walkers and wheelchairs for the elderly. Although the symbols in the sanctuary affirm a solid commitment to the past, the strength of the tradition is sustained by tasteful renovations and contemporary equipment for all contingencies. The church has been here for a long time, and intends to remain openly accepting to all ages and conditions of people.

Entering the church for worship, visitors are warmly and officially greeted by members wearing permanent name tags. Another member immediately prepares temporary tags for visitors, because names are important and the church is too large (650 members) for the members to be certain that they know all the others. The rooms are plain but comfortable, especially the two floors of classrooms in the "new community building" (dedicated in 1955), where the furniture is functional and the modern educational equipment is actively used and carefully stored.

The church has set aside one room for historical artifacts—which need someone to explain them because they are unmarked, as if seeing and touching were sufficient. A large photograph of fifteen hundred men in a Sunday school class in the early 1920s inspires pleasant controversy: was the class really that big, or did they, as some suggest, gather all the men in town for some special celebration and "make a photo to confuse subsequent generations"? Pastors are listed, although only a few of the early leaders have portraits or photographs. But the centerpiece of one wall is a colorful needlepoint quilt that was given to a previous pastor during his illness, then appreciatively returned by his family after his death.

Members have refurbished several gathering places with sturdy Early American furniture to provide a sense of welcome without losing formality. The building reflects a church membership that takes pride in its heritage, lives within its means, and enjoys a bright, contemporary setting for its life together.

CHURCH MEMBERS

The church members, reflecting their community, are drawn primarily from families in business or farming. Their educational background suggests some diversity: a third have no education beyond high school, a third have some college education, and one in five has a graduate degree. Most are married, with full-time employment in their own business or profession, or serve as administrators, managers, and technicians, earning well by community standards.

The pastor, Ben Hill, speaks of the strong lay leadership that guides the policies and activities of West Street Christian Church. The church is rich with talented and committed members. Although the pastor pleasantly notes that the church "no longer has a monopoly on the doctors and lawyers" in town, it still provides a comfortable familiarity for a disproportionate number of leaders from every segment of the community. As these community leaders jokingly recall the actions of former boards to remove their pastors, they reinforce the strong, positive relationship between lay and clergy leaders that characterizes their current style.

Members say that their pastors offer excellent preaching and leadership in both church and community. They take equal pride in the reputation of their church music—the best! Ben Hill and his associate, Ann Tudor Sparks, are experienced professionals who are widely respected throughout the area. As a team they have clearly delineated areas of responsibility and enjoy a collegial relationship in decisions and assignments. One church member, who teased the pastors that they had not grown up in Tipton, said the church was "lucky to attract such good leaders."

In their theological orientation, members range from evangelical to liberal, with most considered moderate.[1] They show unusually strong ties with the Disciples of Christ, perhaps because the denominational seminary is in a nearby city and Ann Sparks serves on its board of trustees. Both pastors, however, feel that the congregation is too complacent about world missions and insufficiently concerned about current social issues that face the church in this community.

CHURCH PROGRAM: VALUES IN ACTION

West Street Church has put its primary energy and resources into programs of worship and education, especially for families and youth. Some of the oldest and strongest church memories (supported by historical photographs) honor the impact of these programs on current church leaders when they were young—and they intend to maintain their traditions. Remembering their own experiences, they recall that "in the 1930s this was the place to meet," and say (with a twinkle), "In the 1950s this was the most romantic church in town." The pastors may struggle to develop programs in evangelism and world mission, but for children and families there is no absence of activities, from Sunday school to scouting, reaching everyone from preschoolers to the elderly.

Anytime during the week there is life in the church building. Only as a formality for Sunday morning are the street doors opened, because everybody knows that the daily routine traffic flows through the other door by the parking lot, then scatters in all directions. During the day there are programs for small children and occasional meetings like the Christian Women's Fellowship. In the afternoon the place explodes with youth activities, and evenings are devoted to a variety of church and community group activities.

One evening each quarter the church takes over the building for a well-choreographed combination of fellowship and planning: first dinner, then program, and finally committee meetings. The sequence provides for the personal contact and organizational efficiency that the members assume in their church and embody in their lives.

Although West Street Christian Church is comfortable with its community, members believe they can make the community a better place to live if, as they say, "we can reach people who *really* need help." Their social ministries have clear, strong roots in their Christian heritage. They point to a history of responding to challenges and developing substantial programs that dates from the last century. By these programs they have tried to relieve the pressures and develop the strengths of people who have been marginalized and alienated by society.

To reach this goal, they developed a variety of ministries from educational programs to medical care, hoping to reach the full spread of citizens, from long-term residents to migrant families. In recent years these programs took shape through the Tipton County Ministerial Association. Both pastors and lay leaders say that this ecumenical witness is "the best expression of our social ministry."

THE MUSTARD SEED MINISTRY

There is something natural, perhaps inevitable, about the social ministry initiated by the West Street Christian Church from the resources provided by the Church and Community Project. In their community study, church members found people who had problems that were insoluble through existing social agencies. They knew some of these people personally, and they recognized others who faced similar conditions.

Church members wanted to help people to stand on their own feet "through the development of life skills, relationships, and long-term strategies." To reach this goal they envisioned a strong program of personal counseling between people who needed assistance and church volunteers, managed by a single paid, professional staff person. Their project design reflected the high value they place on freedom of opportunity. With a strong belief in self-reliance, they wanted to provide help while allowing individuals to make their own decisions for living their own private lives.

NATURAL PARTNERS

The members of the Tipton County Ministerial Association were natural partners for this new ministry. Along with West Street Christian Church, these included their two downtown neighbors, the Kemp United Methodist and First Presbyterian churches, and the more rural Hobbs Christian Church. Also active in the ministerial association and naturally included were two other ecumenical partners—St. John the Baptist Catholic Church and the Sisters of St. Joseph Motherhouse.

St. John's Church and school are located on the east side among the homes of the craftsmen and working people who have given

Tipton a reputation for a high quality of labor leadership. The Sisters of St. Joseph, a century-old order proudly professing to do "anything a woman can do," has pioneered ministries of caring for people with food, hospitality, medical attention, and especially education. Although the six congregations were represented in the ministerial alliance, working together in this new ministry offered the first opportunity for many members to be inside one another's buildings—and they loved it!

ORGANIZING THE MUSTARD SEED

With each church represented by its pastor and two lay delegates, the partners developed a ministry board to determine policy, hire staff, generate funds, review and evaluate program, and oversee the Mustard Seed. The board operates through active committees on public relations, fund-raising, and volunteers. They also have an advisory committee of specialists such as social workers, lawyers, agency representatives, and other resource people who assist in developing policy and working with clients. Like West Street Church, the Mustard Seed is unified by a structure of clear roles, task accountability, and due process.

In its first three years of operation the Mustard Seed has been remarkably successful. It has provided intense help for fifty families, and has made more than two hundred referrals for other kinds of assistance. With a reputation that gives the organization access to resources in community businesses and agencies, it has raised more than $20,000 annually. It has the official support of member congregations, strong backing of the local media, and a positive image in the minds of significant community leaders.

UNEXPECTED CONTROVERSY

Early in the life of the Mustard Seed, the board naively fell into a controversy that would challenge the stability and future of the ministry. One of its clients, who had a green card for medical care because she was receiving welfare, took her fever-ridden daughter to a local doctor's office for attention. His receptionist refused the mother and suggested that she visit the local clinic, where modest payments were required. Lacking funds, the mother bathed her daughter in cool cloths all night, and the next morning she took her to a doctor in a larger nearby town, where she received attention on her green card.

When the director of the Mustard Seed was informed of this problem, spontaneously she gathered a few board members who wrote a memo to participating churches, asking that members inquire if their doctor would treat such a patient. The memo reported that welfare recipients had difficulty receiving medical attention from private doctors in Tipton. The board members did not intend to indict all doctors, but they hoped that an open discussion would resolve this problem.

Because the memo was not completed until Friday, it was not used in some churches and was only quoted in others. But Kemp United Methodist Church inserted the memo in its Sunday bulletin, and that was sufficient to incite a response. One physician was so incensed at the "attack" that he posted the memo in a prominent place (in the men's room for physicians) at the community hospital.

Instead of being silenced, the leaders of the Mustard Seed continued their plan for a public forum where doctors and other citizens could discuss the issue. The meeting had its stormy moments, but in the end everyone seemed to better understand the others: the Mustard Seed leaders understood why the doctors felt that it was easier to refer welfare patients to other clinics or treat them without charge ("Too much red tape with a green card!"); and the physicians understood the Mustard Seed concern and accepted a plan for one agency to be responsible for a fair distribution of welfare patients among community doctors. Although the encounter seemed to end amicably, the incident apparently cost the Mustard Seed some financial support at the time. Even a year later, a few residual feelings remained.

This experience reminded the board of the deep value that the community places on self-reliance and financial independence for both doctors and other citizens. The community supports the Mustard Seed for its stated purpose of helping needy individuals with temporary assistance. The doctors reflect similar values when they reject federal assistance for themselves or the community. Although the Mustard Seed could briefly raise the problem, neither the ministry nor its supporting churches were prepared to sustain a dialogue on systemic questions, such as long-term solutions to the gaps in medical care for the community.

COMMUNITY VALUES
IN THE MUSTARD SEED MINISTRY

West Street Christian Church seems uniquely positioned to be the midwife for this particular ministry in Tipton. In the Mustard Seed we see the indelible stamp of a Pillar church, as we shall consider below. Beyond one congregation, this ministry is a testimony to the pervasive influence of particular values in this mid-American agricultural and business community. On the one hand, the church people care about individual freedoms and independent families, but on the other hand, they also respond to human need with an ecumenical spirit through a strong voluntary organization. The leaders of the Mustard Seed know their community, and put its best values to work.

PILLAR CHURCH: THE SHAPE OF MINISTRY

Although the Mustard Seed is a special product of the committed Christian leaders in Tipton, their model of ministry provides an excellent example of Pillar church leadership.

Sense of Responsibility

Leaders of Pillar churches can build solid programs on a strong sense of Christian civic responsibility. Anchored in a place, with resources and status, the Pillar accepts the obligations of leadership to look out for the welfare of the community. Such congregations have a geographic, parish sense of ministry—they are the concerned Christian presence in that community, or in their area of a larger metropolis.

The Mustard Seed ministry grew from community studies that showed individuals and families who were falling between the cracks of established service agencies. While others may have been aware of the problems, the West Street Church had the power to act, and used its resources responsibly. One of the favorite symbols of the West Street Church is a giant oak tree in its yard, suggesting the sheltering strength it offers to the community.

Like the great oak, Pillar churches shelter a variety of community groups that use their facilities for meetings and activities. The Irvington United Methodist Church in Indianapolis is another example, with its large Tudor building housing programs for groups from preschoolers to senior citizens, from spiritual enrichment to community organization.

In announcing weekly activities, Pillar church bulletins often make no clear distinction between the women's association and WIC (a federally funded program), between scouting and choir practice, since such distinctions would deprive members of practicing their civic responsibility of providing ministries to the whole community. Hope Presbyterian Church in Springfield, Illinois, has redesigned its outreach ministry to incorporate and support three social agencies that share the church facilities.

Leaders of Pillar churches can help members feel more involved in social ministries merely by seeking additional financial support and volunteers for programs that are already using church buildings. With encouragement, these can be quasi-ministries of the church even if they are sponsored by community agencies.

Congregational Strength

Pillar churches are usually large enough to have an active church program, a well-maintained building, and at least one ordained professional leader. Even in a community of a few hundred people, Pillar churches stand tall. The town of Burnettsville, Indiana, for example, has fewer residents than West Street Church has members. The First Baptist Church there may appear small, but it supports a pastor and full program through sacrificial giving and part-time arrangements. The church leaders may be pushed for resources, but they still feel in control of their own future and responsible for their community, body and soul.

Further, communities come to depend on the good judgment of Pillar churches and trust the programs they sponsor. The first year of the Mustard Seed seemed especially auspicious when its sponsors won a $20,000 grant from the new Tipton County Foundation. The foundation considered the Mustard Seed, with its roots in West Street and the partner churches, to be a solid and caring program that would establish a positive community perception of the foundation itself.

West Street's depth of resources and pride in its clergy produce a life-style that is typical in Pillar churches. Since most Pillars are large or medium-sized congregations, they tend to have a relatively low sense of group intimacy and more limited participation in their decision making.[2] Although they expect professional quality leadership from both clergy and lay leaders, their organizational procedures move more slowly than in smaller churches. Leaders should not be surprised that Pillar churches take longer to make decisions, and they depend more on staff to prepare materials and suggest a course of action.

In a typical dilemma, one large congregation was stymied for months when the two experts they consulted gave them contradictory advice. Another congregation took a full year of committee work to decide to hire a community organizer to "help us determine the direction of our program." Pillar church committees tend to study an issue longer, gather more information, recognize more options, and arrive at more comprehensive recommendations. When they act, their actions bear the stamp of the Pillar church style.

Church Partners

Pillar churches are second only to Prophet churches in the number of partners they recruit for ministry, but they go about it differently. Whereas Prophets gather community organizations and agencies as allies in a campaign, Pillars are more inclined to attract other churches to join in a common ministry.[3] Approaching others from a characteristic sense of strength, Pillar church leaders extend an opportunity to join them in service. They do not ask others to assume their broad sense of civic responsibility, but simply to share in ministry.

For the leaders of the Mustard Seed, the interfaith dynamic of their experience is its most satisfying aspect. Like most Pillar churches, West Street finds this ecumenical dimension a more effective vehicle for community concerns and an implied confirmation of their leadership in the community. Without diminishing their denominational commitments, Pillar church leaders often provide significant ecumenical leadership.

Pillar churches frequently treat social agencies differently from the way they approach other churches. In informal networks of helping professionals, pastors often associate with staff members of social agencies to identify areas of community need or to resolve difficult counseling situations. But in organizing church-based social ministries, Pillars serve as flagships that gather a fleet of other churches to share in developing their ministries. Pillar church leaders may utilize the skills of professional agencies, but they are especially gifted to organize ministry with other churches that share their concerns.

Liberal, yet Conservative

Pillar churches play havoc with stereotypes that assume a direct connection between Christian faith and social attitudes.[4] Since these congregations draw disproportionately from community leaders who have reached higher educational and income levels, we are not surprised that Pillar church members are comfortably liberal and moderate in their theological convictions.

But contrary to what we might expect when we look at the rock-solid structures that house these congregations, when compared with other churches Pillars feel least bound by tradition and more willing to respond to contemporary trends. As community leaders, they may take tradition for granted and, in their civic concerns, feel a responsibility to keep in touch with current issues and community problems.

When we compare their views on social issues, however, Pillar churches are significantly more conservative than others. Despite their liberal to moderate theology and their sensitivity to current trends, they resist suggestions to change the world. When Pillar churches confront social concerns, typically they are not convinced that faith requires the church to take a corporate position on justice issues, and are less inclined to actually take such stands.

Leaders can help Pillar churches develop ministries that assist people who are really in need to get on their feet again, but they face inherent resistance to sweeping changes in social, political, or economic systems. Since Pillars attract members from relatively higher affluence and authority, their affirmation of the status quo reflects their confidence in society and their disinterest in significant changes. As a safety net, the Mustard Seed accurately reflects the high priority the community places on individual rights, and therefore emphasizes the self-help aspects of assisting people only until they can do it for themselves.

In comparison with the crisis orientation of Prophets and Survivors, Pillar churches maintain their composure. Situated at the center of community life, they feel no imminent threat to their own existence and often are seen as a rock of stability through times of trial. Yet Pillar churches are not unmoved by conditions of oppression and injustice. As we shall see below, when they are convinced that some aspect of the system is failing, Pillar church leaders can arouse the church to a righteous campaign to give all people their rights and opportunities.

Righteous Indignation

Belying the stereotype of perpetual complacency, Pillar churches can become aggressively involved in social change when they believe that social, economic, or political institutions are not treating people equally or functioning properly. Although, as we noted above, members usually have confidence in these systems and resist corporate social action for systemic changes, leaders can mobilize the righteous anger of the Pillar church into powerful social action when members believe that the basic societal institutions are unfair or dysfunctional.

Westminster Presbyterian Church, a Pillar in Peoria, Illinois, was aroused by its perception that the school board was insensitive to the needs of teenage mothers. Like West Street Church, it engaged the system briefly, but decided to support an alternative program after an initial encounter. HANDS, a justice ministry for the deaf in Chicago, is based in Ridge Lutheran Church, a neighborhood Pillar with a reputation of advocating for American Sign Language in church, community, and denominational meetings. In the larger community, HANDS continues to advocate essential changes in existing systems to make them more responsive to the limitations and possibilities of the deaf and hearing-impaired. Toward this end the ministry has addressed issues of legislation, funding, accommodations, and simple courtesy in medical care, public transportation, police protection, employment opportunities, food services, and other basic necessities of life.

The encounter between the Mustard Seed and the doctors in Tipton reflects the pattern of many Pillar churches when they challenge existing systems. Members of the Mustard Seed board were offended and angered when a basic community institution, the medical care system, failed to accommodate a citizen in a personal crisis. Without carefully considering all the consequences of their action, ministry leaders announced a public meeting to talk with medical leaders to learn why the system seemed to have failed a citizen. Some doctors, as professionals who operate the system, in turn were offended that lay people should question their institutional procedures.

Value commitments were clearly in conflict, with the ministry leaders concerned about the neglect of a citizen on welfare and the physicians seeking to justify their decision while protecting the autonomy of their medical system. In the clash of values, the community standing of both church leaders and doctors seemed threatened. In the midst of public dialogue, the doctors adopted a procedure that seemed fair to these participants, and the churches resumed their typically comfortable relationship with the community. Memories of the event continue to spark discussion, but no one seems ready to reopen the dialogue on the adequacy of health care in the community. Once aroused, Pillar churches seem willing to challenge a particular injustice briefly, but without the energy and determination more typical of a Prophet church.

The Negative Image

Like all church images, the Pillar has a negative side when it becomes ingrown, defensive, and preoccupied with its own concerns. Sometimes the negative image of the Pillar church seems even more pronounced when, with all the resources at its disposal, it turns its back on the community, builds barriers against easy dialogue, and withdraws into an inwardly focused consciousness.

In such a fortress mentality, a Pillar church sees itself as a haven of purity against a sea of sin, standing strong against those issues the congregation perceives as evil, such as gay and lesbian life-styles, substance abuse, overindulgent parents, and romantic welfare programs. With its causes raised like banners and its castle gates open for refuge from the world, the withdrawn Pillar church may gain wide recognition, gather significant wealth, attract new members, and become a thriving institution. From the neighborhood perspective, it appears inaccessible, uncooperative, and disinterested in efforts toward ministry for its immediate community.

Comprehensive Programs

Leaders of Pillar churches have the opportunity to use their resources to move out and challenge significant community problems.

As Pillar churches make community studies, they typically demand more detail, include more options, and take longer to complete them than other churches. In the end they often attempt to make a comprehensive response to an identified need. In Kokomo, Indiana, a Pillar church developed a program to attack adult illiteracy for an unemployed population throughout the county. In Indianapolis a Pillar simply assumed that it could bridge racial and cultural differences in a diverse residential community.

In choosing a target population—such as adult illiterates, confused elderly, or a racially changing community—church leaders can often meet many layers of need at the same time through a multifaceted program. The Mustard Seed attempts counseling, education, job placement, family care, medical attention, temporary shelter, and whatever else the individual or family might need to get up on their feet again. Along with finding the resources, Pillar churches at their best combine a comprehensive vision of the issues with the courage to put their convictions into action.

BUILDING ON PILLAR CHURCH STRENGTHS

Endowed with a wealth of civic responsibility, Pillar churches can mobilize significant resources to meet personal needs and maintain community stability. Pillar churches want everything done well, believing in organizational effectiveness through strong voluntary leadership and professional staff. Pillar church leaders have the best of both worlds—advice from professionals in community social agencies and organizational partnerships with neighboring congregations. Their community studies are thorough and their recommendations comprehensive.

Although theologically liberal to moderate, socially they maintain stability and are inclined to support the status quo. But when members are concerned that a community institution is unfair to citizens or dysfunctional in performing its duties, Pillar church leaders can mobilize a righteous anger, at least briefly. These churches build strong programs on the congregation's commitment to the welfare of the whole community. Pillars are quietly but firmly resolved to do their duty as they understand it.

3 The Pilgrim Church: The Story of Immanuel Lutheran Church

T he Pilgrim church is rooted in a people and a tradition. Many Pilgrim congregations were founded by immigrants and grew up in early cultural enclaves. Some move from one community to another as their people move. Others, like Immanuel Lutheran Church, remain in the old neighborhood and reach out to shelter new groups, helping them to find a viable place in American society.

EDGEWATER

Like many Chicago communities, Edgewater encompasses a wide variety of people and neighborhoods. Along the eastern edge are high-rise lakefront apartment buildings along Sheridan Road; a block inland from them runs the Winthrop-Kenmore Corridor, a low-income, arson-ridden strip now in the throes of redevelopment. To the west, Clark Street's historic Scandinavian flavor now mingles with Middle Eastern, Hispanic, and other elements.

The neighborhood north of Senn High School is quiet, shady, and crowded. Near the school, large apartment buildings scatter among the houses like punctuation in a long sentence. The streets are narrow and one-way, bordered with parked cars and running children. Two or three blocks to the north, large old single-family homes appear too big for the narrow lots. The houses are well kept, and the yards are clipped and flowered. Among the children out of school and the adults sitting on front steps are a variety of complexions:

some Hispanic faces, some apparently Indian or Pakistani, some east Asian, some African and African American. The local elementary school serves children with sixteen different native languages. Ten years ago the neighborhood was 70 percent white; now it is half white and half other races.

On Elmdale Avenue, marking the border between the single-family homes and the higher density buildings, stands Immanuel Lutheran Church. Across the street is a city-owned play yard, which reaches into an unmarked empty lot before adjoining the high school campus. Many Chicago neighborhoods would envy that stretch of open space.

The church is tall, brick, and stately, in a wide U shape with a square tower at one inner corner. Beneath the trees on the recessed front lawn, two spare, modernistic metal columns support a sign-board announcing the services, including Holy Eucharist at 10:30 on Sunday mornings. Behind the sign, three large old bells sit by the walk, inviting the curious observer to search for stories on their ancient bronze surfaces. Now darkened with age, they still bear Swedish inscriptions that few current members can decipher. Near the bells, a hand-lettered sign marks the home of a day program for the handicapped. The ancient bells that once pealed in the Swedish tongue, the contemporary call to worship and the Holy Eucharist, and the homemade sign extending care to those in need, together show the heart of this congregation, worn openly on its sleeve.

THE IMMANUEL LUTHERAN CONGREGATION

The brochure calls Immanuel "An Historic Church Whose Best Days Are Tomorrow." Fewer than a third of the members now are of Scandinavian heritage, though most still are white and of European descent. The pastor's efforts to draw in other people have yielded a few Hispanic members, a few Southeast Asians, and a few blacks. About half the members are married (somewhat fewer than the average for most congregations), and around 30 percent are single and have never married (somewhat more than the average). Forty percent are college graduates; about the same number are employed full-time, and about the same are retired.

The new people who are coming to the church, like the current members, are mostly white and of European background. But they are younger, many in their thirties. They come looking for relationships, say church leaders, and Immanuel has a strong sense of being a family. The pastor, Charles McGowan, adds that these young adults are seeking their own identity, their own place in life and in society, through the church. Many are drawn by the music, art, and other gifts of the church exercised especially in worship; some come for opportunities to serve in outreach ministries.

The church works hard at assimilating newcomers. A six-week membership class emphasizes "orientation, not catechesis," say church leaders, and the Outreach Committee provides sponsors to befriend new members. Ninety percent of Immanuel's worshipers stay for the coffee hour following the service, and members tell of their delight at seeing a new young man sitting at "the old men's table." Social groups organized by age cohort reach out to embrace new members.

ADOPTING INTO THE HOUSEHOLD

In 1979 the church began a partnership with a fledgling congregation of ethnic Chinese immigrants, primarily from Southeast Asia. Responding to an initiative by the synod, Immanuel opened its building to the Lutheran Chinese Christian Church. This new church, composed primarily of refugees from Indochina, shared space, fellowship, and occasional worship with the Immanuel congregation for eight years. In 1987 the Chinese group moved to a building in the heart of New Chinatown in the nearby Uptown community.

During the time that the two groups shared the church building, the two pastors worked hard to create opportunities for sharing and mutual learning. The two congregations worshiped together periodically, and the pastors carefully incorporated both styles and cultures into the liturgy. Immanuel members smile as they recall fellowship suppers with "sweet and sour Swedish meatballs," and they speak of the loss they felt when the Chinese church moved out of the building. The two groups continued to work in partnership, including cosponsorship of Project New Start, a program to assist Chinese immigrants with language training and job placement, begun through the Church and Community Project.

The partnership with the Chinese church seemed natural to Immanuel in light of its own immigrant history. In their planning materials for Project New Start, members recalled that their church "was organized in 1853 to meet the worship and social service needs of the large contingent of Swedish Lutherans who were coming to Chicago at the time," and they speak of the hardships faced by those pioneers. In light of that background, they say, "Our cooperation with the 'Boat People' from Southeast Asia . . . has its link with Immanuel's early immigrant history." Further cementing this tie, they tell of the daughter of Immanuel's first pastor, who "traveled to the mission fields in China in the late nineteenth century to sow the seeds of Christianity."

A COMMON JOURNEY OF FAITH

These two Pilgrim congregations express their shared theology in terms of the Exodus story. Within that motif, they remember God's covenant with the people of Israel in Genesis 12:1–2: "Go from your country and your kindred and your father's house to the land that I will show you. I will make of you a great nation, and I will bless you." Both congregations identify with the story.

"Immanuel's Exodus from Sweden began as Chicago was in its infancy," they say. "These people came to the city via the waterways of the world to find their hopes and dreams fulfilled in the new country." Paralleling that experience, they say, "the Chinese also had an Exodus experience; however, it was one born out of war and conflict. 'The Boat People,' many of whom comprise the [Chinese] congregation, had to leave or they would lose their lives." Finally they add, "From the wilderness of sin to the promised land, we the people of God come and go, as we seek to be faithful to our God who calls us to further images of the Exodus through times of testing and times of faith."

More recently, Immanuel hosted a congregation of the Bible Fellowship Evangelical Church of Eritrea, an immigrant group from northeastern Africa that shared its building for thirteen months before deciding to accept the sponsorship of the Lutheran Church Missouri Synod. Pastor McGowan and other leaders speak rather wistfully of the Eritreans' departure, saying that "it would have been nice to keep them as a part of the ELCA." For this Pilgrim church, new cultural groups enrich its faith experience.

WORSHIP AND CONGREGATIONAL LIFE

Rooted deeply in the Lutheran tradition, this Pilgrim congregation gathers in a tall, stately sanctuary for worship. They have treasured a "high church" style of worship for as long as anyone can recall—a legacy of their roots in the state church of Sweden—and their conversation often returns to this central experience. One relatively recent member whose personal background is with another cultural group speaks gratefully of the occasional use of incense, which was not accepted in the church he previously attended. And even as they live out their heritage in liturgy, it surrounds them vividly in sun-cast colors: stained-glass windows in the sanctuary and side chapel portray their immigrant story and mark their role in founding early Lutheran benevolent institutions.

This is an active church. Members participate often in church activities besides worship, and most belong to a number of organizations, groups, and committees within the church. Symbolically, they point to the number of members who participate visibly in the worship services. Leaders point out proudly that, with an average of 110 worshipers, they have a choir of eighteen. Laypersons serve Communion and read the scriptures, as well as serving as acolytes, ushers, and greeters. The Altar Guild prepares the altar for the Lord's Supper each week. Members are pleased to see people of all ages up front at the altar, and they are excited that senior women serve as deacons. In addition, the Banquet Bearers take Communion to shut-in or sick members.

A network of organized social groups helps knit together this church family. With names like the Minglers and the Odds and Ends, these age-based groups offer close fellowship to longtime members and reach out to draw in new ones. There is a group for every stage of life or family development, including a seniors' fellowship, a program for mothers and young children, and the Immanuel chapter of the Women of the Evangelical Lutheran Church in America (WELCA). In addition, forty-seven members have committed themselves to be part of the Caring Network. These volunteers develop relationships with shut-ins or persons in crisis through visits, phone calls, and cards. Members call it "caring for each other within the family."

COMMUNITY OUTREACH

This is also a congregation with a strong concern for outreach, and their evangelism is embedded in ministries of service. They are especially eager to reach children and youth. The church sponsors a tutoring program, for example, in which members assist fifteen to twenty grade school children in reading and math. Church members place a strong value on education, and a number of them serve as volunteer tutors.

Immanuel has a long tradition of youth ministry, and members make a special effort to mentor young people as leaders in the programs. Their goal is to plant seeds within the kids they reach, recognizing that the church may not see the fruits until much later, if at all. Their grammar school and high school youth groups draw primarily from the neighborhood, and they speak enthusiastically about their vacation Bible school. It was, in fact, through the Bible school that they developed their connection with the Eritrean church. Through initial contacts with a few individuals, they saw the needs of the Eritrean community and of this congregation in particular, and they extended an invitation to the Bible Fellowship church to use their facilities.

The parish nurse is seen as an outreach ministry, as well. Among other things, she conducts the Together Program, which includes three classes per week for young children and their caregivers. Moms and Tots meets once a week, and Friends School meets twice. The nurse describes the program as similar to a preschool class, with the parents or other caregivers staying to participate with the children.

The church has its own food pantry and also supports Care for Real, the community food pantry and clothing source. Immanuel maintains strong ecumenical relationships, especially with the neighboring Temple Emmanuel and St. Gertrude's Catholic Church. It is active in the Organization of the Northeast, the local community organization. Furthermore, it has made its building available to a number of social service groups: the Augustana Center for Developmentally Disabled Adults, Thresholds (a post–psychiatric-care support group), Alcoholics Anonymous, and Al-Anon.

Leaders emphasize that their current outreach ministries are continuing expressions of their historic commitments. By example, they point out that Immanuel Church helped to found Augustana College (now in Rock Island, Illinois) and Book Concern a century ago—and now they sponsor a tutoring program. Similarly, they helped to start Augustana Hospital of Chicago long ago—and now they support a parish nurse. Over the years the church has launched eight daughter congregations—and now they have helped the new Chinese and Eritrean churches. They say they are "building on the past to move into the future," through responding to their awareness of need in the community in ways that treat the whole person.

PROJECT NEW START

A clear example of that continuity was Project New Start, the Church and Community project that Immanuel began in partnership with the Chinese church. The congregation's historical and theological motivations for assisting that new group found a new opportunity when the synod recommended them for Church and Community participation. But its leaders point out that this was an unusual step, as well—a white congregation undertaking to directly affect the lives of another ethnic group.

Project New Start was born of the two congregations' shared concern for the needs of Southeast Asian immigrants. The most active element of the program was English classes offered at the Chinese church's building in Uptown. Children, adults, and grandparents attended the classes, which were taught by volunteers from Immanuel and, for a while, by a staff person hired by New Start. The classes also provided orientation to life in an American city, including such skills as making change and using public transportation. In addition, the New Start staff person and the Chinese pastor frequently counseled individuals in crisis or need.

The committee's original goals included job placement and eventually small business development, but the latter never came about. New Start did place some immigrants in service jobs, particularly as caregivers to homebound elderly in the Immanuel congregation. After three years the program foundered, primarily because of the difficulty of finding a long-term staff person who could speak Mandarin and Cantonese along with English, and the lack of funding to support a permanent staff person if they found one. The English classes continue, and the two congregations still seek ways to minister to this immigrant population.

The Heart of Immanuel Church

The glue that holds the Immanuel congregation together, then, is a mixture of three elements, all arising from their cultural heritage: their history, their sense of family, and their distinctive worship.

Leaders refer often to Immanuel's particular history and its legacy in the Swedish Lutheran tradition. Pastor McGowan, though not Scandinavian himself, cherishes this history and teaches it in the new-member classes. He says the newcomers respond positively and with interest. Charles adds, though, that the people "are not stuck on the Swedish tradition." A pastor who served from 1919 to 1949 made a conscious effort to broaden the congregation's horizon, and freed it from an inappropriately strong tie to its single founding group. As is apparent above, the heritage lives on in the congregation's motivations and areas of focus for outreach ministry, in the worship style, and in the symbols that surround them every Sunday.

In worship the members live out their particular heritage of high worship and pietistic faith. The pastor describes their background as "evangelical Catholic," rooted in a traditional, sacramental Lutheran theology and a formal sense of ritual. And on issues like conversion and biblical literalism, the members of Immanuel tend to be more liberal than average congregations. Yet Charles also sees a deep strain of pietism within the members, which weaves in and out of their worship. One of the congregation's favorite hymns is "How Great Thou Art," popularized by George Beverly Shea during Billy Graham evangelistic crusades, and they enjoy a number of other "old gospel thumpers" as well.

In fact, part of their bond of commonality with the Chinese congregation lies in their identification with the deep evangelical piety of its pastor. Though the tongue is different, the language and expressions are familiar; and their joint worship often included old-time gospel hymns loved by both groups.

The sense of family is part of the legacy as well, and it colors their conversation and shapes their programs. Their fellowship groups, based on life stages, draw the bounds of family comfortably close around the members. The Caring Network, with nearly half the active congregation participating, is explicitly intended to care for each other "within the family," and participants tell ready stories of ways members look out for each other, such as checking on elderly members who fail to answer the phone.

But they are quick to add that their sense of family includes both the church family and their "extended family." They speak in the same family images when they talk of reaching out to others around them, as they do when they tell of caring for "our living treasures who are scores old in the tradition of the church." In that sense of extended family—and remembering their own immigrant roots—they have embraced the Chinese, the Eritreans, children and youth in the neighborhood, and all who need them.

This Pilgrim congregation, then, carries its cultural heritage as a living legacy on which it builds today's ministry. But the culture lives on not in the surface expressions—not in quaint Swedish phrases, blue and yellow flags, or Midsummer holidays. Even the "sweet and sour Swedish meatballs" are a token remnant used in fun and to build bridges with its partner.

Much more significantly, the Immanuel congregation carries its heritage in its ministry values and commitments. The heartbeat of their shared faith and culture over a century ago was not in language, but in mission to immigrants in need, a sense of caring for each other as family—and for strangers as extended family, and the power and beauty of shared worship. In that core of its identity, Immanuel's cultural history feeds the fires of its contemporary ministry.

Immanuel Church "doesn't say no to anyone," say its leaders. In Charles McGowan's words, "We have to be open. We never know when the Spirit is going to send new people. The stranger among us must be welcomed."

PILGRIM CHURCH: THE SHAPE OF MINISTRY

While Immanuel Church is richly unique, as is every church, its story illustrates a number of the characteristics of the Pilgrim image.

Faith, Culture, and a Caring Family

Pilgrim churches are rooted in a people. Their cultural history colors their sense of identity, like a patterned window refracting the sun. Even today, more than 135 years after Immanuel's founding, the congregation still values their Swedish heritage. It surrounds them in stained glass; it lives in their worship and fellowship.

Some Pilgrim congregations are recent immigrants; they wear their tradition openly in language, customs, and continuing family ties with the homeland. For second- or third-generation Pilgrims like Immanuel, the outward signs of their history may be evident only in occasional annual events and a few old jokes. But the heritage dwells more deeply within the congregation. The members of Immanuel identify their cherished worship style with their strong Scandinavian Lutheran tradition. That worship nourishes them, binds them together, and reminds them of who they are.

Typical of Pilgrim congregations, they also talk often about being a family. These culture-based congregations tend to have a strong sense of bonding as a church family. A thick web of congregational caring has sustained Immanuel ever since the days when the modern group's ancestors were strangers together in a new land.

The sense of history and of family are common in Pilgrim churches. For pastors and lay leaders, the good news is that history need not be a millstone, and family need not be exclusive. Leaders who recognize the power of the congregation's history can use that power to energize contemporary ministry—as Charles McGowan appealed to Immanuel to live out its historic values in new outreach ministries to recent immigrant groups.

Similarly, the Pilgrim congregation's strong sense of caring for each other within the family can provide a base for reaching out to adopt others. Members of Immanuel are quite conscious of this extended family sense, and they pursue it actively in their efforts at reaching and assimilating newcomers. Both history and family, operating without guidance, can limit a church's vision and growth. But used wisely by leaders who understand the congregation and are willing to risk pushing its frontiers, history and family provide deep resources for new outreach ministry.

Working to Make a Place in Society

Most Pilgrims were born among marginalized populations, and through long years they have worked to help "our people" establish themselves in American society. As a result, Pilgrim churches and their members are often among the most active in social ministries—

though they rarely think of themselves as political activists.[1] Immanuel Church does not often lead community battles against social injustice (nor does it withdraw from such issues). But a large number of members spend time in ministries of service and compassion—from the Caring Network of nearly fifty people to the preschool classes, food pantry, and parish nurse.

This high level of involvement is typical of Pilgrim congregations, and it is a great strength on which they can build. When church leaders recognize and celebrate the members' ministries, they can encourage others to become involved as well, and can help them grow through their experiences.[2]

Because of their people's historical efforts to move from the margins to the mainstream, Pilgrim churches most often build social ministries that are oriented toward long-term improvement in people's lives and opportunities. Educational ministries are common—and are usually done well. Youth are important in Immanuel's outreach efforts, and the church is particularly proud of its tutoring program. Project New Start, with its English language classes and job skills training, sought in immediate, practical ways to help ethnic Chinese immigrants make their way in the city of Chicago.

Another Pilgrim congregation, with a very different cultural history but the same concern for long-term improvement in its people's opportunities, is the Riverside Park United Methodist Church in Indianapolis. This small African-American congregation created an after-school tutoring program similar to Immanuel's. The leaders talk frequently about their concern for young black men—their people, their youth, their future. Through the tutoring ministry they hope to intervene during childhood in order to open a broader future than street life for black youth (both boys and girls). From a variety of origins, Pilgrims journey along similar paths and come to common concerns—especially for their youth.

Liberal Views and Moderate Faith

Members of Pilgrim churches generally hold the most liberal social attitudes of all congregations, and they often share with Prophet churches the highest comprehension of the systemic dimensions of social problems.[3] The social views of these two images are quite close—but they live out those values in very different styles.

Leaders who recognize their congregation's style can help them to develop the most effective ministries.

While Prophet churches, fueled by righteous anger, feel deeply called to challenge systems, Pilgrims take a different approach. Pilgrim congregations have learned by their history how dysfunctional those systems are, and they work hard to help marginalized people make their place in society in spite of them. While the Prophet is trying to tear down a barrier, its Pilgrim neighbor is trying to build a bridge over it.

Although their social views are generally liberal, most Pilgrim congregations carry a moderate theology.[4] The faith of Immanuel's members is an amalgam of liberal and pietistic elements. On issues like conversion and biblical literalism their views are generally more liberal than average congregations. The pastor describes the style of their faith as "evangelical Catholic," and he finds a clear strain of pietism in their common language and their love for the old gospel hymns. The product is a shared faith that avoids liberal or conservative extremes by incorporating diverse elements.

Traditional Leaders

Charles McGowan recognizes and appreciates those varied elements of the congregation's theology. In significant ways he represents the kind of leader Pilgrim churches generally seek: one who honors and represents their tradition at its best, as they value it. He is also well aware that often, though not always, that means the pastor shares the congregation's ethnic background. Charles is the first pastor in this church's century-plus history who is not Swedish, he says, and the prospect bothered him more than it did them. He confesses to some trepidation when the parish called him, wondering whether he would be accepted.

But culture is more than ethnicity, and a Pilgrim pastor needs more than an ethnic birthright. What is important to Pilgrims is that their pastor honor and embody their tradition *as they perceive and value it.* The Immanuel congregation quickly found that Charles knows and celebrates the significant elements of their rich heritage as they do— their history, including a history of outreach ministry, their strong sense of family care, and their distinctive liturgical tradition. He also pushes them to reach beyond their heritage—to risk for the sake of the gospel. Held firmly by strong and shared roots, they respond.

Only three miles from Immanuel, and very similar in character, another Pilgrim congregation of Swedish heritage illustrates how a pastor and parish with one image in common can form a good match even though they differ in other ways. North Park Covenant Church, as many other congregations, sees in itself not one but two primary images. Members express this mixed identity as "Pillar-Pilgrim"—or, as some people say it, as a "Post-Pilgrim Pillar." Yet they speak with love and enthusiasm of a pastor who served the church during the 1960s, who frequently challenged social injustice in classic prophetic style.

When members of North Park were asked how a Pillar-Pilgrim church could get along so well with a Prophet pastor for over a decade, they responded, "He always preached from the Bible. Somehow he brought it around to social issues, but he always preached from the Bible."

And there he touched the central nerve of the tradition. For Covenanters share a history in which the Bible has been the only creed, and they test every teaching by asking, "Where is it written?" In his strong biblical base this pastor represented their tradition as they valued it. There was also a prophetic element within the congregation itself, which he nourished and which nourished him; but he was a beloved and effective pastor to the whole church. He was not just a Prophet, but a Prophet-Pilgrim, and he pastored a Pillar-Pilgrim church. He found, as have others, that a strong, shared cultural-faith tradition can enable a pastor to lead a congregation into new areas of witness.

Partners Within the Family

In general, Pilgrim churches are slow in partnering. When they do, they tend to form partnerships within their extended family— through denominational ties, cultural networks, or neighborhood connections. Pilgrims care more about who people are than what they do. When Immanuel Church turned to its partner congregation in developing Project New Start, it was not because it needed a Chinese church in order to build a ministry to Chinese people. Rather, it chose to minister to Chinese people because the Chinese congregation was already its partner.

There are a variety of family partnerships for Pilgrim leaders to explore. When the Riverside Park church sought a partner for its tutoring program, it turned to a nearby Baptist church that shared both its neighborhood and its African American culture. Other Pilgrim congregations have raised significant funds for community ministries from sister congregations within the denominational family. Building on trusted relationships, the Pilgrim church can mobilize human and financial resources to help make ministry possible.

Changing Communities, Changing Cultures

Most Pilgrim churches that were born in concentrated ghettos of particular cultural groups have now seen waves of immigration wash through the community, leaving an increasing variety of human cultures behind. The Edgewater community has long since ceased to be a Swedish enclave, as one group after another has moved through the neighborhood. In fact, Edgewater is no longer the turf of any one group. Here, as in many changing city communities, a variety of cultural groups now occupy a single neighborhood—living on the same blocks, their children in the same school, but speaking different languages in the home.

In the face of changes like these, some Pilgrim churches pull up stakes and move to other neighborhoods as their people move. This is true especially of first-generation Pilgrims, who share the strongest ties with their country of origin, the freshest struggle for a place in American society, and a primary language other than English. Symbolically, they move their tabernacle as their people journey on.

By the second or third generation, many Pilgrim congregations have incorporated members from outside the original ethnic group, have set down roots in the community, and reflect other images along with their Pilgrim heritage. Thus North Park Church has become a Pillar as well as a Pilgrim, and the same is true of Immanuel. Along with its Pilgrim characteristics, Immanuel shows its Pillar nature in its insistence on the professional quality of its leadership and worship, and in its sense of community responsibility that is not limited to particular ethnic groups even though it springs from that well. Other second- or third-generation Pilgrims may take on Servant or Prophet characteristics.

These older Pilgrims are more likely to remain in the neighborhood through successive population changes, and they often adopt new cultural groups into their sphere of ministry. Their view of the community is broadened by their cultural heritage, so that they see in the newcomers' experience their own parents' or grandparents' stories, and they reach out to help. Thus the Immanuel congregation, remembering their own immigrant story, welcomed the Chinese group. They offered them a place to meet, broke bread with them, and—perhaps most significantly—found occasions to share with them in worship. When the Eritrean church needed a home, Immanuel opened its building once again.

Another mixed neighborhood is Little Village, on Chicago's West Side. The community is now primarily Hispanic, though the earlier residents were of European backgrounds. The Millard Congregational United Church of Christ represents the history of both the church and the community: the longtime members are of Slavic descent and the newer ones are Hispanic. Incorporated in a single congregation, they talk of their shared excitement in worship that is accompanied by both an organ and mariachi instruments.

Immanuel and Millard illustrate two different responses by Pilgrim congregations that remain in changing neighborhoods. At Millard, Hispanics and Anglos share together as members of a single congregation, celebrating their different cultures along with their common faith. Immanuel's pattern, on the other hand, is perhaps more usual—creating or adopting separate congregations with their own cultural integrity.

The Negative Image

There is a third kind of response to the community, which represents a less healthy expression of this image. Some Pilgrim congregations remain so bound by their own cultural identity that they are unable to reach out beyond it. They tend to their own people, carefully defined, separate from the rest of the community. If they have joined the cultural and economic mainstream, they may be hostile toward other groups or simply oblivious to them. Those who remain in the minority and continue to experience forms of oppression may reinforce dead-end divisions rather than creating bridges. For these negative Pilgrims, their journey has limited their ministry, not broadened it.

BUILDING ON PILGRIM CHURCH STRENGTHS

Pilgrim leaders have much to celebrate. These churches have a strong and steady commitment to walk with a group of people through the long, slow process of making a viable place in our competitive society. Especially in city neighborhoods (though there are some Pilgrims in rural communities), Pilgrim congregations are tutoring children, teaching English to immigrants, and faithfully supporting the needs of marginalized groups. Their strong, moderate faith grounds their liberal social views in the longer story of God's work among humankind, and their instinctive understanding of the value of culture enables them to reach out to people who are different from them.

For Pilgrims, tradition is a source of energy to reach out, not a wall to hide behind. Rooted in the past and with a vision for the future, they continue their journey of faith and witness.

We are not lost through wandering,
  For by your light we come;
And we are still God's people,
  The journey is our home.[5]

4 The Survivor Church: The Story of the Evangelical Covenant Church of South Chicago

Although the Survivor church may appear fragile to outsiders, it brings surprising energy to the overwhelming problems it faces. Often located in declining neighborhoods, Survivors are surrounded by real and complex social problems—as South Chicago Covenant Church has outlasted the steel mills that once sustained its community. This small congregation has learned to take risks in order to reach out to a changing population around them. Sustained by their strong faith, they persist in responding to the needs they see in the best ways they can.

THE EAST SIDE

The East Side is an island. A long, narrow island, it is bounded by Lake Michigan and the Indiana state line on the east, the Calumet River and the S.C.&S. Railroad on the west. At the south is another railroad line and a forest preserve. To the north, the river bends around to reach the lake, cutting off the East Side from its nearest neighbor, known as the Bush. The Calumet hosts a major shipping terminal, and towering cranes and lifts have staked successive claims along its banks.

Bridges are the threads that connect the East Side to the city at the north and west. When the drawbridges go up, no one enters or leaves the island. The same happens at railroad crossings along the lower half of the long western border. On these occasions, even ambulances cannot get into or out of the East Side.

From the river's mouth to the far southwest end, the East Side is anchored by huge steel mills, most now cold and quiet. Wisconsin Steel is dead (in the words of residents). U.S. Steel has cut back from ten thousand employees to a few hundred. Republic is mostly closed and has removed half its buildings. At one point in recent years, unemployment in this historically steel-dependent community reached over 20 percent. "Steel built this area," says one resident. "Now it's gone, and the area doesn't know what to do with itself." Still lingering is a feisty blue-collar independence—perhaps partly inherited from the Slavic ancestors of the longtime residents. People believe in the American system: you stand on your own two feet. "You can make it somehow."

More recently the community has felt threatened by a proposal by the city to develop a major new airport adjacent to the East Side. While none of their property would be affected directly, residents speak at length and with animation about their sense of uncertainty and displacement. To make matters worse, they do not expect that they will get any of the new jobs to be created—only specialists will qualify for them.

The old-timers in the East Side are of European ethnic backgrounds, and many neighbors have known each other since high school, forty years ago. But in recent years the influx has been Hispanic. In 1980 the community was 87 percent Anglo and 13 percent Hispanic; by 1990 the Hispanic population had grown to 40 percent. Yet the businesses along the thriving blocks of Ewing Avenue and 106th Street all have European names. Farther north on Ewing are a few small Hispanic shops: Gomez's Fruit Market, Robles Supermercado, an occasional storefront restaurant.

THE EVANGELICAL COVENANT CHURCH
OF SOUTH CHICAGO

In the 100th block of Avenue L, just off Ewing Avenue, frame and asphalt-shingle-sided houses crowd on narrow lots, with scarcely any daylight between them. Most are two stories, many with two front doors signaling two apartments. When the sewers were put in, years ago, the streets were raised several feet above the foundations of the homes, and most yards still slope down sharply from the sidewalk. The homes are in good repair, for the most part—some with new siding, a few with old, peeling paint.

At the north end, dominating the whole block, an elevated expressway crosses diagonally, high over the intersection. Not more than two hundred feet from its crossing sits a small white frame church with red-painted brick foundation and entrance. Over the door, an ancient electric sign in the shape of a cross no longer lights. But the doors are brand new, with brass handles, and there are signs all across the front:

EVANGELICAL COVENANT CHURCH.
THE FRIENDLY CHURCH. EST. NOV. 1883.

WELCOME TO THE EVANGELICAL COVENANT CHURCH
OF SOUTH CHICAGO

EVANGELICAL COVENANT CHURCH.
GLORIFYING JESUS! 1991

EVANGELICAL COVENANT CHURCH.
AROUND THE WORLD FOR GOD.

Built by Swedes and sustained by Slavs, the church has never been large. At its peak in 1940 it had around 160 members. For the last two decades the membership has never topped seventy; between thirty and forty adults now gather for worship on Sundays. Few members bring few dollars, and the people have never been wealthy. The church has often faced the threat of closing.

THE CONGREGATION

The current board members reflect the historical profile of the community and congregation in their national backgrounds: Serbian, German, Scottish, Croatian, French. As early residents had no cars, they came to the neighborhood church they could walk to. Now all the new arrivals—in the church as in the community—are second-generation Hispanics. In fact, the census tract immediately around the church is 63 percent Hispanic. Reflecting the variety of their own backgrounds, church leaders emphasize that the Hispanics are diverse: they come from a number of different Central and South American countries.

About a quarter of the worshiping congregation now are Hispanic. When these neighbors first began coming, the church held two services, one for the Hispanics and one for the Anglos. But in 1989 the two groups began meeting together, and the mix seems to have worked well. Anglo leaders say the newcomers are attracted by the warm welcome they find. One longtime Anglo member says it this way: "We welcome you. Come on in. We don't understand you, we don't know how you feel, but come on in." It is a candid admission of unfamiliarity, and at the same time an invitation from the heart.

The church has also made some changes to help the newcomers feel more at home. Worshipers often clap hands now when they sing, and tambourines add to the spirit. "Other churches would have a fit about the tambourines," they say; in fact, "this church would have had a fit earlier." Making Christmas plans this year, the board sought to create a service that both Anglos and Hispanics would enjoy. Significantly, they chose to include some of the Hispanic members in the planning process from the beginning. They also printed the announcement of the service in Spanish as well as English.

The newer members, different as they are in culture, are drawn to this congregation not only by the warm welcome, but also by two deeply significant life experiences they share with the Anglos. The first is the constant fight to survive, which new and old residents share with their neighborhood and their church. And the second— the energy that sustains their survival—is a personal commitment to Jesus Christ. "When you have people with a sincere relationship with Jesus Christ," say the leaders, "it draws people in." This is the enlivening commitment of this small but determined congregation, and it is the message they feel compelled to take to their neighbors.

Their survival experience, their deep and personal faith, and their evangelistic zeal are all intertwined. Their faith carries them through threats and troubles, and in turn they want to share that faith with other struggling neighbors. Through everything, the soul of the church remains constant. Even as the church changes its ways, customs, and music to accommodate the new group in their midst, members emphasize that "the church itself doesn't change: its belief, its faith." When asked what that unchanging core of belief is, one leader responded on behalf of the group, "God's word: God created. Man sinned. Jesus came. We must believe that Jesus died for our sins, and commit ourselves to the work of God." The Bible is all-important, and members quote it frequently. "Society seems to have moved away from biblical teaching," they say, and they seek to return to that foundation in all they do.

Most of the members live (or have lived) close to the bone in one respect or another—facing financial struggles, frequent layoffs and job searches, personal and family difficulties. Through it all, their faith in Jesus sustains them. Some have histories of severe social and personal problems, such as drugs, alcohol, and physical abuse. "They have come out of it," says one member, "because there really is a Jesus." Leaders emphasize the strength of their prayer life—as individuals, in worship, and in a prayer chain that unites the congregation in support of special needs.

The members' dogged determination to meet the challenges of their lives is reflected in the church's history as well. They readily tell about the fire in 1979 that damaged the church while destroying two houses immediately to ᵗhe north. The north side of the church sustained heavy damage, and the stained-glass windows in that wall were lost. They rebuilt, doing much of the work themselves, and they love to tell the stories of how they reclaimed their church from disaster.

KEEPING THE CHURCH GOING

Like many Survivors, South Chicago is a small church; the leaders all do several different jobs within the church, and they have for years. Board members teach Sunday school, pay the bills, and care for the building—for example, installing the new front doors. They sustain a youth group for junior and senior high school students, and a children's arts and crafts group that meets once a month.

The women's group—traditionally a source of strength in many congregations—has become mostly inactive. As the longtime members aged and the newer women did not fit in, the group disbanded for a while and is now only nominally active. Other traditional ministries remain strong. The Wednesday evening prayer meeting, for example, is important and well attended.

Recently the congregation has organized several "C.A.R.E." groups: "Christ Active, Real, Experience-able." These groups meet weekly, drawing together members with similar family circumstances (young couples or families, for example) for mutual support and growth.

Reaching Out to the Neighborhood

Even as they tend to their inner life and growth, this small congregation continues to reach out in whatever ways they find at the moment—both to carry the life-changing gospel faith they have found, and to sustain the church's own viability. Leaders point out that the old ethnic enclaves from which their members came are now gone. The community is changing rapidly. In the words of one board member, "If churches want to survive, they have to rethink how they're going to survive—how they're going to develop into the neighborhood." And another quickly adds, "This is not our plan. We're doing what God's word tells us to do. The answers to all the world's problems are in God's word, and within the church."

Leaders emphasize the importance of being open to people who are different from them in background and style. "This church is willing to open up to new ideas," they say, "providing that they don't ruin the gospel message." When asked if that openness has helped the church to survive through the years, they respond quickly, "Oh, definitely! Had we stayed the same, we'd be dead." Even though virtually no African Americans live in the East Side (they live across the river to the north), members are pleased that a black woman has begun coming to the church and may become a member. A resident of the WellSpring House (the transitional home for abused women that the church sponsors), this woman finds commonality with the congregation, they believe, in a "faith that overcomes the world's divisions."

South Chicago Covenant also participates in a community ecumenical group that sponsors joint services on special days. What is important to them is the commonality of a faith based on scripture. Beyond that, they gladly honor their neighbors' preferences to attend other churches, and they talk particularly about their acceptance of the Catholic faith. After years of skeptical distance across an evangelical Protestant–Catholic divide, they now say, "We're finally saying we do believe in the same things." Board members say this openness is part of the heritage of the Evangelical Covenant denomination to which they belong, and it also has a missional purpose for them. "If all the churches agreed and worked together," they say, "there's no telling what we could do in the community."

For as deep as their own faith roots reach, their conviction is just as deep that "the church is a place where God's will should be shown to the rest of the neighborhood." They know their own limitations as human beings and as a small congregation, but they are determined to do what they can. "We're not supposed to see or do the whole plan," they say. "But there is a part for this church to do for the community."

In the late 1970s the congregation shared a parish social worker with two other Covenant churches in Chicago. In 1979–80 they sponsored a holistic health center in the parish house. They began offering English-as-a-second-language classes, and together with other East Side churches and organizations they established an emergency food pantry. During the early 1980s the church rented a storefront on Ewing Avenue near 106th Street, where they offered recreational and educational programs for community children.

In the late 1980s they established the Barnabas Project—an umbrella organization for their nascent efforts to provide decent housing for low-income people. Together with Barnabas, the church rehabbed a two-flat building, named it the Jubilee House, and rented it to two low-income families.

WELLSPRING HOUSE

Over recent years the congregation's involvement in these ministries has shifted somewhat. A decade ago, the pastors carried most of the burden of doing community ministry. The congregation clearly supported the programs, but in practice the pastor (or the social worker) did the hands-on work. As long as the pastor had the vision and the energy for community outreach ministry, the congregation gave its blessing.

By the time they developed the Jubilee House, the congregation were becoming more involved. Members worked on rehabbing the building, and in the process they developed a sense of ownership not only of the property, but also of the ministry. At that point in their life, they joined with the Church and Community Project and began planning the WellSpring House.

WellSpring grew out of their concern for housing and the start they had made with the Jubilee House. Several abused women sought help from the church in finding housing for themselves and their children. As members came to know these families and learned about their struggles firsthand, they resolved to create a safe place for them to live. They found a six-flat apartment building several blocks from the church and turned it into a transitional housing center.

Again, as in the past, the initiative for WellSpring came from the pastors—in this case, a clergy couple with a charismatic style and a burning vision for helping people in crisis. They recruited church members to join them on the committee and enlisted a young Hispanic woman to chair it, but there was no question where the driving energy came from.

The point of testing the congregation's commitment came early in 1989, in the project's first full year. Simmering tensions between the congregation and the pastors boiled over, and the pastors resigned and left the church abruptly. Although the estrangement grew out of broader issues of authority, it inevitably affected WellSpring House. For when the pastors left, the Barnabas Project they had founded also severed itself from the church's sponsorship. In this divorce, the support and custody of WellSpring was in question. Would it become a Barnabas program, or would it remain with the church?

At that point, the congregation spoke up and claimed it. Church leaders—with significant help and support from the associate superintendent of the denomination's Central Conference—formed a new board to oversee WellSpring, including some members who had been involved from the beginning, some new ones, and interested persons from the community. Even as the congregation had made a financial commitment earlier by signing the mortgage on the apartment building, it now reaffirmed its commitment to the ministry and the church's role in it. The members were ready to do "whatever we can do to help people," they said. Having recognized domestic abuse and homelessness as a problem for some of their neighbors, they were committed to do what they could to address the problem.

Speaking of the women who seek shelter at WellSpring House, one church leader said, "These people not only need help, but they need to learn how to help themselves—to stand on their own two feet." The blue-collar, old ethnic belief in the American way is strong. And even as abused women struggle for viable lives, so the WellSpring project itself has faced obstacles. "WellSpring takes more than wanting it," said one of the church members. "It takes commitment, time, and other resources." The building has not always been full, money is scarce, and the director resigned after a year of twenty-four-hour responsibility. It took a number of months to replace her.

The church will help keep the project going as long as it can, with a resignation to the will of God if it cannot. "With all the help that was offered to us through the Church and Community Project," said one board member, "God was saying, 'Keep it going as long as it's working.' If there are not enough resources, God will be saying, 'It's not something I want you to be in anymore.'" Another one adds, "God doesn't do everything for people. He expects people to do it. They wouldn't learn anything if he did it all."

MOVING INTO THE FUTURE

Most recently, the church has entered a new stage in its outreach to the community: the church board voted unanimously to create a new Board of Outreach. In doing so, they are institutionalizing their outreach in the very structure of the church in a way they have never done before, and they take the step very seriously. They carefully considered appropriate membership on the new board, accountability to the church executive board, and similar constitutional questions before taking final action.

But the genesis of the Board of Outreach was a characteristic, spontaneous response to the call of God. Church leaders tell how God raised up an evangelist among them, a Hispanic woman. She will chair the new board, and the board will provide a legitimate channel for her ministry. There is no question where this congregation's priorities are. In the words of one board member, "It's important to follow rules and procedures, but we never put that ahead of what God wants. If it's a choice between the Bible and the constitution, the Bible is going to win." In their new Board of Outreach, they have created a way to honor both. The biblical faith that has sustained them throughout their lives must be shared with others.

It remains to be seen whether the new Board of Outreach will become the liaison to the WellSpring board. All the questions about

WellSpring's viability and the church's resources to sustain it remain alive. And the will of God comes first, with the constitution second. When the Lord wanted these people to create a safe home for abused families, they made a way to do it. When God raised up an evangelist, they created a board to enable her ministry. They will continue listening to the Almighty, and responding in the best ways they can.

It would have been the easy thing to do, confess these survivors, to close the church long ago. And had it not been for the determination of the people, they would have done so. But they have kept going through over a hundred years of precarious existence in their island community because of their firm belief that there is something that God wants this church to do.

"Sometimes we get down on ourselves," they say. "We look at how small we are—you would think God's purpose would be more grand. But literally hundreds, thousands of people have come through this church and been influenced by the gospel message. We have taken the gospel to people, we have been faithful—so God has also been faithful and allowed the church to keep on."

And their advice for other Survivor churches? "Tell them, 'Never give up! Persevere!'" And to the one who perseveres, a crown will be given.

SURVIVOR CHURCH: THE SHAPE OF MINISTRY

In the experience of South Chicago Covenant and other, similar congregations we can see some of the characteristics—and yes, the strengths—of the Survivor church.

Overwhelmed by Hardships

Survivor congregations and their members feel overwhelmed by problems beyond their control. Like most Survivor churches, South Chicago Covenant has clung to life in the face of hardships: declining numbers, shaky budgets, and a disastrous fire. Many of the members have survived trouble or crisis in their personal lives. Unemployment, economic uncertainty, even chemical and physical abuse—few in this congregation are untouched.

Yet somehow the struggles they have weathered hold them together and keep them going. Survivors' crises become, paradoxically, a resource on which their leaders can draw, for they produce unity and energy for reaching out to other strugglers. Their endurance becomes a positive element of their identity. One pastor reflected her Survivor congregation's quietly persistent attitude this way: Whatever comes, they always say, "Well, we've made it through worse than this before"—and then they get to work.

Survivor Communities

Even as the church and the members face persistent threats to their existence, so does the community. Most Survivors reach out to neighbors who are as threatened as they are. Not surprisingly, many dwell in aging, declining urban neighborhoods like the East Side. The conditions in the community affect the viability of the church: South Chicago Covenant is in part a product of its isolated, struggling, steel-dependent community.

Even as industrial decline has colored the context in which South Chicago Covenant ministers, widespread family decay has shaped the Indianapolis neighborhood that is home to the West Park Christian Church, another Survivor congregation. In the blocks around the church, small frame bungalows house transitional, often dysfunctional families. Few biologically related households have remained intact in this neighborhood; single or remarried parents do their best to raise mix-and-match families on low incomes.

In this context, West Park Church has tried to respond to the needs of young adolescents through a drop-in program in the church basement one night a week. As they try to work with these teens and their families, program leaders find their own energies sapped by the pervasive relational dysfunction around them in the community. Yet, true to the Survivor image, they keep on trying.

Making a Dent

In the face of such internal and external obstacles, the key to the strength of the Survivor is quiet determination. Time and again leaders will find that, rather than withdraw from the neighborhood and its problems, the Survivor congregation tries to do something—to make even a small dent in the needs the people see.

They know they cannot do everything, but they can do something. The handful of survivors at South Chicago could not remedy the broad need for low-income housing in their community, but they could fix up one building to help two families. They could not eliminate the gangs that roamed their neighborhood, but they could invite a dozen children at a time into a storefront after school. They could not stop family abuse, but they could give shelter to a few women and their children.

Conservative, Socially Caring, and Close-Knit

Survivors persist because their faith carries them through. Most Survivor churches are evangelical or moderate in their theology.[1] These are high-commitment congregations: the members' strong personal faith sustains them through their own struggles, and they share a passionate dedication to their church. Relatively few Survivor churches are theologically liberal.

As the South Chicago congregation illustrates, an evangelical theology seems to provide a faith for struggling people. The emphases on a personal relationship with Jesus Christ and on biblical authority offer a simplicity, structure, and power that can give strength to those who are deprived of other advantages. The people at South Chicago Covenant live their evangelical faith every day; it breathes in their lives, their language, their prayers.

There are theologically moderate Survivor congregations too, who steadfastly keep on going because of their deep and unshakable faith. For some, survival has become part of their heritage, shared from one generation to the next with a quiet constancy. As a member of one Presbyterian Survivor church put it, "This church has a long and proud history of surviving adversity."

Despite their conservative or moderate theology, Survivors typically have relatively liberal social attitudes, and most are active in community outreach ministries.[2] Members of Survivor churches know firsthand the kinds of social realities that may be only headlines or statistics to some other congregations. Pillars, for example (who share with Servants the most conservative social views), are often composed of middle-class members with ties to local economic institutions, living in fairly stable neighborhoods. Even with deep commitments to ministries of compassion, they often cannot know the realities of economic injustice and month-to-month subsistence as Survivors know them.

Survivor congregations are also close-knit groups.[3] Their typically small size and their crisis style create strong bonds. Usually a small core of active leaders are responsible for making most of the decisions, and all the members know what is going on in the church. South Chicago Covenant lives in a comfortable tension between constitutional government and response to the Spirit. Because they are so few and the key leaders know the congregation so well, they were able to create the new Board of Outreach without fear of resistance. The congregation's closeness enables them to risk, perhaps more readily than other congregations might.

This closeness also enables the Survivor congregation to take public stands at times on social issues.[4] Survivors operate by consensus rather than by votes. Pastors and other leaders who know the congregation well know what issues they can address and what they must leave alone. But on issues on which they agree, Survivors can take a stand—and gain strength and confidence in the process.

Overworked Leaders

At most Survivor churches, the pastor and active lay leaders feel overworked and spiritually undernourished. South Chicago Covenant is typical of many Survivor churches: a handful of leaders are doing virtually everything—the church board, the Sunday school, neighborhood outreach, even maintenance of the building. In response to this, the current pastor at South Chicago, Rick Sutter, emphasizes spiritual growth within the congregation. Most important to them, he teaches the word of God. He is convinced that changes will come in the lives of the members as they apply the word.

In particular, Rick has begun a careful program to build strong bonds of fellowship and mutual support within the church. In the past, he says, the members have been somewhat isolated from each other. Now, with the theme "Making disciples of Jesus through equipping the body, by the power of the Spirit," they have formed several care groups that will become permanent cells within the congregation—a group for young married couples, for example, and one for singles. "These people give and give," says Rick, and they need to be fed: "I'd just like to tie 'em up and feed 'em." In the care groups, as well as in worship and sermons, the people are fed.

Not far away on the South Side of Chicago is an even smaller Survivor church that has faced the same problem. At Cornell Baptist

Church, near the University of Chicago, Sanjay Patel's strategy for pastoral care has been similar to Rick Sutter's. When Sanjay came to Cornell midway through the development of their Church and Community project, this handful of deeply committed Christians were worn thin by overwork and trauma. Their previous pastor had left under tense and unhappy circumstances, and the congregation was trying to work through their grief while sustaining both the church and a large after-school tutoring program. With only about twenty adult members, everyone had to shoulder part of the burden, and no one could rest.

When Sanjay came, he quickly sensed both their dedication and their fatigue. Like Rick, Sanjay responded by concentrating on the congregation's spiritual nourishment. Little by little he began building them up, comforting them with the message that they did not have to do everything at once. In fact, he encouraged some people to lay down their volunteer burdens, insisting that work done for the Lord should bring joy—and if it doesn't, one probably should be doing something different. And, little by little, the weight began to lift. By the time Sanjay had been there two years, the mood of the leaders had lightened and they were sounding more like a Pillar church than a Survivor. No longer overwhelmed by their troubles, with confidence born of faith they talked broadly about their responsibility for the welfare of their community.

Few Partnerships

Survivor congregations are often reluctant to form partnerships for community ministry. Although they would seem to need help the most, they try to go it alone. South Chicago Covenant incorporated a few individuals on the WellSpring board who happened to belong to other churches, but neither those churches nor any other organizations share corporately in the responsibility for WellSpring. Cornell Baptist sought contributions and volunteers from a few Southern Baptist congregations out of state, but their only continuing partnership is with the local elementary school from which the students in their tutoring program come.

It may seem threatening to Survivors to risk partnering with stronger groups, or they may simply be conditioned by long years of making it on their own. Whatever the reasons, Survivors are often loners.

The Negative Image

Not all Survivors fit the active, responsive profile drawn here. A Survivor church may become so self-absorbed with its own problems that it withdraws from the world outside. Like black holes in space—dark stars that pull light in toward the source, rather than shining it outward—these congregations exhaust their members and all who try to work with them. They draw in energy and focus it so completely on the church that little ministry escapes their walls.

Other Survivors give up: they either close the church or fall into a kind of paralysis in which they are unable to make the simplest decisions. Even planning the annual Christmas service may seem an impossible task to a group that has lost its will to live. And some of these churches may not be salvageable. There is a time for closing a church, with celebration for its lifetime of ministry, and moving on.

But some withdrawn Survivors can reorient themselves, with the help of skilled leadership. Pastors and lay leaders of these churches should beware the temptation to push them too far too fast—to insist that they instantly become something new. Withdrawn Survivors are vulnerable to believing that if they cannot do everything, they cannot do anything. Sensitive leaders can encourage them to begin with one step in reaching out—to take an initial risk in faith. Survivors may not be able to do much, but they can do *something;* and each step in ministry will shape and strengthen them for the next.

Building on Survivor Church Strengths

Survivor congregations can be sources of help for individuals and catalysts for social change when they resolve to do their part in the struggle against overwhelming needs, using their crises to mobilize energy and resources for ministry. Survivors and their leaders seem built for crisis ministries. Their commitments are deep and unshakable, and they are able to enlist others to join them in the struggle. Often Survivors are particularly good at recruiting volunteers and raising money, apparently out of nowhere. Their backs seem against the wall, and they are often tired. Yet they will not give up. They know the Lord has something for them to do, and—by the grace of God—they do it.

5 The Prophet Church: The Stories of Shalom United Church of Christ and Edwin Ray United Methodist Church

Prophet churches are assertive, restless, and ready to risk all for their vision of God's reign. Both of our examples, Shalom and Edwin Ray, believing in a God of justice who expects the church to encourage social righteousness, use crisis as a creative opportunity for community change. Shalom has chosen a broad-based prophetic witness as an alternative to a more affluent congregational style. Edwin Ray, an older church with fewer resources, has turned its urban limitations into the challenge of providing housing opportunities.

Biblical Prophet: Shalom Church (UCC)

Bible study can be dangerous. In the spring of 1987 the participants in a long-term Bible study within a large suburban, mainline congregation in the university community of West Lafayette, Indiana, reached a breaking point between the values and commitments they found in the Bible and the relative comfort and affluence of their surroundings. The problem came to a head for study leaders when church officers denied their recommendation to alter the church's priorities. From their studies of the prophets and the witness of Jesus, Bible class participants believed that the church should give as much to mission as it spent on itself—and their church was well known for the care of its building and the beauty of its sanctuary.

As the tensions increased, a few leaders of the Bible class quietly discussed among themselves the possibility of organizing their own congregation, where they could more freely and completely express their faith. When they met with the regional executive for the United Church of Christ, he supported their proposal, based on their commitments to a prophetic witness and a congregational heritage in the United Church of Christ. A small group of members from the class continued to meet in the evenings into the summer, to clarify their mission and define their standards. They envisioned a gathering of committed Christians, where members engaged in mission in their lives and church resources were divided equally between their congregation and the larger church mission.

On the first Sunday evening of August 1987, with the pain and drama of birth, forty-five people from the Bible study group and their families gathered in worship as a new congregation in a chapel rented from another church. Out of a climate of conflict, they selected the name of Shalom Church. *Shalom* is a Hebrew word for peace, which carries the connotations of wholeness and well-being, therefore suggesting the right relationships essential for personal fulfillment and social justice. Shalom represented their "dream for a more just society and a world at peace under the ultimate reign of God."[1] They also liked the name because it was a little out of the ordinary.

FROM WORSHIP TO ACTION

Worship remains central to this congregation, with recommitment in the liturgy of the Lord's Supper every Sunday. Drawn from teachers, professionals, and graduate students, most of the thirty-six members, twelve children, and a dozen "friends of the church" attend Shalom every week. The total membership has not changed, but about half of the original members have departed and been replaced by new recruits. Because many are younger families with children, they have moved their weekly worship and educational program to more traditional times on Sunday mornings, and have moved the place to more spacious (but still rented) quarters.

In every service of worship the times of recommitment to mission are significant, for Shalom Church sees evidence of faith in active membership support to mission. Most members practice tithing; they generate over $30,000 from eighteen pledging units, with 50 percent of their income used for mission—"and that's first."

More than their money, the church expects of all members that they will be involved in some sort of community ministry or agency, and provides numerous options for the congregation. In food and health care, the members bring supplies for the pantry, find funds for welfare recipients to have prescription drugs, and are personally involved in a neighborhood effort toward lice control. In housing, members have been active in shelter programs, Neighbors in Need, Habitat for Humanity, the Drop-in Center, and the Community Crisis Center. More recently they joined a prison ministry, and have personally helped post-prison rehabilitation. In the midst of spiritual renewal on Sunday morning, there's always a time for reports from members on significant encounters in their weekday ministries.

Although Shalom Church is composed of members who prize their autonomy, as a congregation they have taken corporate stands on open housing, world peace, protection of children, and the inclusiveness of membership in their congregation. They have marched carrying their trademark, life-size puppets, not only in Lafayette, but in the state capital, Indianapolis, to protest the Persian Gulf War, when popular sentiment ran strongly in the other direction. Such commitments reflect the depth of their convictions on contemporary issues, transcending their strong but comparatively minor differences in theology and overcoming their natural reticence toward public displays.

In its search for new expressions of mission, Shalom Church discovered the Lafayette Transitional Housing Center. Sponsored by St. Boniface and St. Thomas Aquinas Catholic churches with seed funding from the Church and Community Project, the Center provides temporary shelter, child care, counseling, and referrals for employment, education, and health needs for homeless families in the community. When Shalom members read about the program in the newspaper, they called to offer their help. Through Shalom's financial support and their business and professional contacts, the transitional housing program moved more rapidly from being a program trying to answer a recognized need to becoming an established social agency. Although the pastor and members of Shalom remain active as needed, their concentrated interest has recently shifted to other ministries now that LTH's early crises have been resolved.

GROWTH PAINS

As a church that acts out its convictions, Shalom has struggled to find appropriate forms for shaping and expressing the faith of its members. In community recognition, Shalom UCC is widely known as the congregation "with the funny name" that has unusually active members who volunteer throughout the community and a faith that's summed up in its regular newspaper ad: "Inclusive worship, Communion every week, working for justice and peace, global awareness." Now, after four years of monumental effort, church leaders are slowly realizing that, although they are well known, their membership is not growing.

After reassessing its situation, Shalom has moved to develop a stronger and more permanent institutional base. In retreats and congregational reflections the members redefined their goals to include the strengthening of personal and spiritual relationships. Through a significant new grant from denominational sources, they secured their first full-time clergyperson early in 1991. Rev. Jane Orr seems uniquely suited to the challenge, since she helped organize a similar congregation in another state for three years as a layperson prior to her seminary education. As pastor to a mission-minded congregation, she finds that her primary role is as a spiritual leader—individually among the members, in the group life of the congregation, and in worship, where they expect her "to preach the prophetic Word of God."

MIXING NEW AND OLD

The pastor reports that several of Shalom's challenges seem rather typical, almost pedestrian, when compared with their high mission goals. Church music has been a problem, partially solved when they found inexpensive hymnals that had inclusive language—a necessity in Shalom's style of communicating. The question of a choir was resolved by an ingenious seasonal emphasis that could be an inspiration for other struggling congregations. The church has an organized choir for only four major liturgical events: World Communion Sunday in October, the Christmas season, Palm Sunday and Easter, and Pentecost in late spring.

Organizing an educational program has not been so easy. Like most small churches, Shalom struggles with class size because its few children are unevenly distributed by age. Curriculum selection is a challenge, since the church has a tradition that encourages groups to study whatever they choose, which creates occasional tensions between those who plan and those who teach. Adults are invited to join covenant groups that study contemporary religious literature; and, naturally, there is an "un-covenant group" (including the pastor), which explores the faith implications in current movies.

Now that it has a pastor and growth goals, the congregation is considering a building. But the structure, like the members, would need to be useful in mission seven days a week. Members are reviewing a plan to share space in the development of a low-income retirement home, but they are also attracted to the vision of a multiservice center that would demand from them a wider range of their gifts in ministry.

As evidenced from the beginning, decision making remains their most pervasive challenge. The church has several planning and program committees that have interim authority to act. Based on its egalitarian past, however, primary decisions are made by a bimonthly meeting of the church board, which is composed of all the adult members. Not majority rule, but consensus is required. Therefore, the most significant decisions are likely to be deferred for full consideration in congregational retreats. The residual problem, they have discovered, is not that too many people want to speak to an issue; rather, they find a few people who remain silent when the issue is discussed and later harbor unresolved feelings after the time of decision has passed. Through these experiences, however, they feel Shalom Church has matured into a supportive and committed Christian community.

Theologically, Shalom members believe that these challenges test and strengthen their faith, individually and together. The congregation has already had an impact far out of proportion to its size. With a priority on understatement, Shalom Church remains intentionally strong and humble.

We honor Shalom Church as evidence that amazing results can happen when a small group opens its Bible study to the power of the Holy Spirit. When we see what these dedicated people have accomplished, we wonder, as they do, why more groups that study the Bible seriously do not begin new churches—and why more people do not join in the joyful disciplines of Shalom Church.

Yet by honoring Shalom, we may put them on a pedestal as some-how different, unlike typical congregations. By making them a spe-cial case, we may increase the distance between us and them, and in that distance we may overlook the disturbing possibility that God may be calling us as well. For that reason we include a second, per-haps more accessible example of a prophetic church.

Prophet by Choice and by Permission: Edwin Ray Church

Edwin Ray Church is located in an Indianapolis neighborhood several blocks away from major traffic streets of the city, a neighbor-hood of single-story frame bungalows individually constructed by European immigrant labor families toward the end of the previous century. Some of the careful craftsmanship has been maintained, but more has been overused and replaced with an odd assortment of makeshift arrangements. Larger homes, now showing multiple mail-boxes, are scattered throughout the neighborhood. Home repairs are spotty. Small trim lawns, exquisite little gardens, and hanging flow-erpots are mixed with bricklike asphalt siding and amateur roof repairs. Freshly painted trim stands next to a derelict home with ply-wood covering the doors and windows. As an older community in the midst of change, this mixed neighborhood resembles many urban areas.

The residents' backgrounds reflect the waves of immigrants who have found shelter here. The older, longtime inhabitants have Ger-man, Irish, and Italian ancestry; their children left the area some years ago. The younger families are usually from Appalachia, close enough that they can return to former homes on weekends. Layers of older and younger populations can be identified by the folding chairs, rocking chairs, and pillows on the porch chairs for the elderly; and by the torn-down autos, pickup trucks, and motorcycles in the yards of the younger families.

Many typical urban problems plague this community, including illiteracy and unemployment, drug use and child abuse, teenage preg-nancy and lack of day care for children or adults. Yet neighbors seem comfortable together: no racial ghettos separate the area, and many

American flags and patriotic symbols decorate these homes, as if they all share a fundamental human solidarity.

OLD EDWIN RAY CHURCH

Edwin Ray has been told it is a dying church in a neighborhood where new members are hard to find. For more than a decade it has defied the predictions of church planners, simply by surviving. Like the community, the struggle of this church is typical of many across the country. Of about sixty members in this congregation, two thirds are more than seventy years old and have been members most of their lives, and most of the rest who attend are related to the older generation.

Unlike many urban churches, most members of this century-old congregation live in the neighborhood. Like many of their neighbors, most church members have no college background, but once earned their living in hourly employment and now are retired on social security and other modest incomes. For an ambitious pastor, this charge would seem to be a disappointment.

Yet the feelings inside the network of members are strongly affirming. With 80 percent attendance on most Sundays, the members of the congregation keep in touch—physically, socially, and spiritually. Their closest friends are members, and they have an almost absolute confidence that church members support one another in troubled times.[2] They recognize that the odds are against their survival, but these "facts" have strengthened, not broken, their spirit. And in the past few years the neighbors have also begun to see the church differently.

Members trace the change to 1985, when Ruth Farr, a lifelong member and retired missionary, chaired a search committee that found a newly ordained pastor who seemed to fit their needs. Through the bishop and at her own request, Rev. Mattie Collins was appointed to this "impossible" situation. The match seemed inspired, and the partnership began immediately. As two former lay missionaries with experience overseas, Mattie and Ruth shared a passion for ministry among the poor and a vision for the community grounded in their faith.

GIDEON'S ARMY

Working with the congregation, Pastor Mattie discovered that church members shared her conservative, evangelical faith and her activist view of the church in the community.[3] Their faith had not been stated in so many words, but it had been acted out through years of caring for one another. Financially, they support the church by giving about 5 percent of their meager incomes, twice the average annual per capita gift in their denomination, with less than half the average annual income.

Furthermore, all the programs of the church were ways of caring, often organized by the leaders of extended families. For example, Betty, whose grandchildren make up most of the Sunday school, is the pivot for Friends and Neighbors, a monthly dinner and community social gathering. The Women's Association, Susan Circle, Circuit Rider Class, urban 4-H Club, and Mothers' Day Out are all associated with particular figures in congregational history, and the line between members and neighbors is intentionally unclear. For years members had been practicing this faith within the congregation; Pastor Mattie simply refocused that faith into community action.

Mattie Collins's leadership style made the difference. From the handicapped and shut-ins to the active teenagers, from the "We'll pray for you" elderly to the street people at the pantry, the answer to what makes things work was the same: Pastor Mattie loves everyone. Early and late, she has made the church credible by her honesty of speech and her problem-solving way of loving. Pastor Mattie not only lives her faith, she helps her members articulate the faith they are living with her. They have, in her words, gained confidence that God can use them in the things they are already doing, and more. She calls it "experiencing the wholeness of word and deed." She calls them Gideon's army.

"THY KINGDOM COME"

Even while the congregation struggles to survive, Mattie talks of transforming the neighborhood to become more like "the kingdom of God," where, as she says, "the operative dynamic is love and the character is peace and justice"—or simply, in the words of Jesus, "Thy kingdom come, thy will be done." To this end Pastor Mattie is said to work forty hours a week as caregiver in her parish, and to "give a second forty hours a week" to building networks and connections among school leaders, agencies, and neighborhood service organizations. Ruth Farr puts it theologically, saying, "When we see a need and have the resources to respond, that's the call of God for us." To both Mattie and Ruth, the resources of the Church and Community Project seemed God's special call for answering human need through working for God's will on earth.

In confidence ("common faith") that God can use its people, this struggling congregation has become the pivot for a massive assault on poor and deteriorating neighborhood housing. With the backing of Church and Community seed funds, and using community development skills that they learned at the Ecumenical Institute and practiced in the mission field, Pastor Mattie and her husband, Josh, have generated more than half a million dollars in the past two years for the Fountain Square Church and Community Project, to rebuild and renovate substandard neighborhood housing. Like a general staff in the war room, Josh and his assistants from VISTA and Methodist volunteer missions map the location of the next houses to be changed and chart the necessary tools, materials, and volunteers for each task.

While church members prepare meals and provide a base for ministry, volunteers come from far and wide—from the communicant classes and fellowship groups of churches throughout the city, from college classes and fraternal groups, from professionals with expertise and court probationers doing community service, and from neighborhood youth who are learning salable skills. It takes a lot of little blocks of time to change this tough old neighborhood. Every month more than a thousand hours of volunteer labor pour into the community, mostly on Saturdays, to revive the homes physically and the neighborhood spiritually. In the process, the volunteers are themselves transformed.

CONTAGIOUS FAITH

How can small and dying Edwin Ray have an impact so much larger than itself? Leadership, to be sure—the mix of Ruth, Mattie, Josh, and

all the others like Betty who make it happen. Symbolic of the excitement of this ministry, Jim and Peggy Sue Cook have been inspired to
return from their suburban retirement to live next door and work as
parish missionaries in this urban ministry. They provide a continuity
of care for individuals who need special attention and for persistent
parish problems that would otherwise consume the pastor's time.
Each of these people is a visionary, in his or her own way responding
to God's call.

The contagious faith of Edwin Ray Church has given many members new freedom and renewal of spirit—not, says Pastor Mattie, in
spite of its precarious situation, but because of it: "We are able to risk
because we have faced death as a church and a neighborhood, and
found the meaning of faith in the resurrection of our continuing life
together." Then she adds, with a disarming smile, "Of course, not
everyone works with us. Some members join us by choice, and others
simply give us their permission." After a moment of reflection she
confides, "That's one difference between Josh and myself: Josh works
best with those who are with us; and I love them all, even if they
don't know they are with us, yet."

Although very different in many ways, both Shalom and Edwin
Ray are alive with the prophetic spirit of God, serving and, even
more, transforming this world here and now.

PROPHET CHURCH:
THE SHAPE OF MINISTRY

Although prophetic churches take special pride in being unique,
they have some common characteristics in the way they engage in
social ministries.

Vision of the Kingdom

For members of Prophet churches, the promises of God's coming
reign are vivid, almost tangible, if only we all begin now. When the
vision seems that real, they are restless, assertive, and ready to risk
whatever is necessary to follow where God calls.

Where Survivors are reactive to the difficulties they face, Prophet
church leaders are proactive—seeing in every crisis the opportunity
for advancing God's realm. Run-down homes signal community

decline, but in their repair the prophetic church hopes to unite a community through brickwork, roofing, and new paint. When a victimized woman brings vivid consciousness of widespread spousal abuse, sheltering her family is a step toward housing for all.

The impatience of a Prophet is often experienced by others as aggressive behavior. Consequently they are are often independent, even hostile, toward social, political, and religious institutions that they feel are insensitive. The denominational executive who helped midwife Shalom Church determined that the vision of the young Bible study group could no longer be contained within the routines of an established congregation.

Carrying this vivid vision and its resulting sense of urgency, prophetic ministries are often vehicles for innovative solutions to old problems. In Springfield, Illinois, for example, Hope Presbyterian Church expanded and redesigned its proposed building to provide working space and facilities for organizational cooperation for three community agencies serving children, families, and the elderly. Although this unusual ministry put them at odds with denominational funding sources, they are convinced that this comprehensive ministry should become more typical throughout the church. In joining their church with other agencies in a common building, their joint ministry operates seven days a week, with new sensitivity to a variety of social concerns and with ample opportunities for volunteers.

Coalition Allies and Partners

Prophet church leaders are particularly resourceful in relationships with other, nonchurch groups. Clearly they make more allies in their chosen causes.[4] And these are unique when compared with partnerships of other congregations. Prophetic churches are the least likely to stay within familiar networks and the most likely to develop functional and creative coalitions with service agencies, schools, hospitals, businesses, banks, and community organizations. When partners are allies in the fight for the cause at hand, temporary coalitions are built for those specific purposes.

Shalom Church hardly missed a beat as it joined with two Catholic parishes that had formed Lafayette Transitional Housing, but its interest in the project declined when the initial crises were successfully negotiated. It workers were off to Neighbors in Need,

Habitat for Humanity, the Community Crisis Center, and numerous other projects on the cutting edge. In the Fountain Square housing program, Josh Collins has allies and liaisons with more than twenty organizations that supply volunteers, financial help, building materials, and other necessities. But the project decisions remain with a core group who lift up the vision of God's reign like a tent to gather the many groups that support their common cause.

Strong Congregational Leaders

Prophetic churches need vigorous leaders who articulate the vision and are ready to withstand the inevitable abuse that comes with suggesting changes. Charismatic or gifted leaders have been associated with such sectarian movements that break from established churches or advocate significant systemic changes. Prophet leaders are graphic in describing community problems, eloquent in envisioning God's coming reign, and urgent in their appeals to action. We have been stirred by their appeals against drug abuse and the alarming increase in teenage pregnancy, spouse abuse and domestic violence, inadequate housing and corruption in city government, and other equally overwhelming community problems.

The solo prophetic leaders who inspire but do not share easily with their constituents consistently have problems, however, in nurturing or yielding leadership. In one church the pastor-prophet was so vivid, even graphic, that others never seemed to express their mission with sufficient fervor, so he remained the only spokesperson. In another, since the lay leaders and even clergy colleagues were never trusted with raising and dispensing the project funds, the solo leader controlled the project by the purse. Not all Prophet leaders are solo singers, but those who are can seem stellar for a time, yet leave little when they are gone.

By contrast, these two Prophet churches share leadership. In Edwin Ray United Methodist Church the charisma begins with Pastor Mattie, her husband, Josh, and Ruth Farr; they share the joyful discipleship through various layers of church and ministry leadership. In a congregation that's not much given to verbal analysis, members of Edwin Ray articulate at length and with clarity the gifts of their beloved leaders.

In Shalom, the role negotiation continues as the new pastor takes her place among the strong people who compose the congregation;

nothing is taken for granted, and nothing denied. Since the congregation makes decisions by consensus, the mantle of leadership falls to those who consistently help members make connections between a dream they share and the particular ministries that are right for each member.

This contrast of types of leadership in Prophet churches makes clear that there is no one style that precipitates or sustains these ministries. In a large African American church, the pastor remains the pivotal figure, although he claims to decentralize decision making in both formal and informal ways. In a small-town Church of the Brethren congregation, the preacher is highly honored, but the board of elders quietly retains its authority. In an inner-city mainline church mission, the fund-raiser has the final say. In a thriving urban Hispanic ministry, the pastor departed when insurgent members on his board challenged his authority. Prophetic leaders must sustain the vision in the midst of the people and pragmatically negotiate a leadership style that works for them.

High-Commitment Members

Members of prophetic congregations show significantly higher levels of church commitment by participating more frequently and providing more financial support than members of other churches.[5] Worship is central in the life of Prophet churches; in both Shalom and Edwin Ray, more than 80 percent of the members attended worship on a typical Sunday. In both situations, their financial support for the work of the church is double their denominational average—an astounding record, especially for the lower-income members of Edwin Ray Church. In both, the members are more involved in every phase of traditional and innovative church activities.

But more, members of Prophet churches take genuine pride in their participation in ministries and mission beyond the congregation. Prophetic churches typically make a high level of community involvement a standard of belonging, and the members are significantly more likely to comply. In Edwin Ray the expectation is voiced in its informal conversation, while the more professional Shalom has written guidelines to help members remember their commitments. Although faith cannot be measured, the faithful show their colors by investing themselves in ministry.

Despite—or perhaps because of—these demands, members feel affirmed by the inner life of the congregation and satisfied with their own decision-making procedures.[6] In Shalom, where educational levels are higher and economic mobility is greater, the members are more critical of decision making. In Edwin Ray the members have outlived their internal feistiness, or have simply grown accustomed to it. Leaders of Prophet churches expect high energy levels, which escalate the commitments of their own people and inspire, and sometimes intimidate, others around them.

Theologically Diverse, Socially Radical

Contrary to some popular misconceptions, these socially active churches are not always theologically liberal. In Prophet churches evangelical, moderate, and liberal theological views appear with equal frequency.[7] In practice, when evangelical congregations become aroused about social issues they feel motivated to act by an authority from God that is not necessarily limited by contemporary social standards, legal restraints, or even personal safety. When Sweet Holy Spirit Baptist Church in Chicago feels that God has called its people to a "street ministry" of public demonstration against crime, drugs, and prostitution, they march at night through the worst areas, to take their message personally "with the protection of the Lord." They are clear about evil, and solid as to the source of their faith.

Liberal churches, on the other hand, are less likely to be located in low-income areas where issues are so stark, and have greater difficulty defining issues with sufficient clarity to mobilize prophetic action. However, although most Prophet churches are not theologically liberal, they hold liberal views on social and political questions. Thus Edwin Ray, with its blue-collar constituency, has developed a far more liberal profile on social issues than the typical congregation either in their community or in their Methodist communion.

Prophet church leaders find that people change their views by hands-on experience. They become more compassionate when they volunteer in ministries that acknowledge their role in oppression, or that introduce them to life-styles of oppressed people. In these experiences they accommodate a variety of theological inconsistencies until the mind can catch up with what the heart already understands.

In this way the prophetic awareness can be supported by all three traditional theological postures. For many prophetic ministries, experiential revelation often precedes rational understanding.

Supporting Justice Ministries

Leaders of Prophet congregations elicit the strongest commitment to justice in their social ministries in two ways. First, prophetic churches are most likely to see that social evils are caused by destructive systems as well as personal deficiencies.[8] When Prophets become concerned about changing the systemic causes for particular social problems, their ministries of service move naturally into advocacy for social justice.

Thus the Westminster Presbyterian Church of Peoria, Illinois, which mixes Prophet with Pillar, began by challenging the school board to retain teen mothers within the system; but when the board was unresponsive, they moved to supporting an alternative system that they hoped the board might adopt in the future. When Hope Church of Springfield realized that denominational regulations denied funding for building church facilities to be shared with social ministries, its leadership created a special task force to challenge the denominational policies.

Second, Prophet church leaders can develop strong congregational positions on advocacy issues when members are sure that such stands are required by their faith in a God of justice. Amazingly, although the members of Shalom Church are professionals who live quite independent lives, as we have seen they are willing to join as a congregation to take corporate stands on open housing, world peace, protection of children, and the inclusive membership in their congregation. Carrying their trademark life-size puppets, they have joined public demonstrations in their own city and in the state capital. Such a church is both a weather vane for significant issues and at times a battering ram against the injustice its people are sure offends Almighty God.

Using Crisis Energy

Although Prophet churches are proactive and Survivor churches are reactive, they both harness the energy of crises. Survivors do their best to cope with each new problem, while Prophets are inclined to translate every individual incident into a larger campaign. Both use crises to demand high levels of commitment and convert community needs into a sense of urgency. The programs and processes they produce are very different, but their energy and loyalty are surprisingly similar.

Some admirers are tempted to make the prophetic church normative for congregational social ministry—a high standard by which other churches are judged poorly. But, as these case studies suggest, the majority of congregations build on other identities to develop their social ministries. Rather, Prophet churches remain the bellwether of denominational social action—sensing the impending crises, generating interest in the issues, and shaping the theological, ethical, and social analyses for subsequent church involvement.

The Negative Dimensions

There are negative forms of the Prophet image too. In their hard-driving, high-energy style, prophetic churches may become enamored of confrontation for its own sake. Adrenalin can be addictive, and some Prophets slip into engaging in the critique without the cause. If the central, motivating vision of God's reign is lost or pushed to the background, the residue may be a behavioral pattern of conflict without theological grounding.

Leadership can be a problem in Prophet churches. In addition to the problems of a solo pastor, noted above, Prophet churches are also vulnerable to sudden shifts of their pastors' interests. On the other hand, some Prophets can get tangled up in trying to remain completely consistent to their own principles. Shalom, for example, is burdened by its commitment to equality and democracy in reaching consensus in decisions; it simply takes a long time.

BUILDING ON PROPHET CHURCH STRENGTHS

With a vivid vision of God's realm, prophetic churches remain restless and impatient with the world as it is. Strong leaders invite high-commitment members to change existing systems to conform with the will of God. In community action, the Prophet church builds pragmatic partnerships and develops coalitional allies to achieve their common ends. Although grounded in all three of our categories of theological persuasion, Prophets are consistently more socially radical. Beyond ministries of service, they join with the alienated and oppressed to advocate for social justice. They may sometimes be in error, but with vision and commitment, they are never in doubt.

6 The Servant Church: The Story of Leet Memorial United Methodist Church

The Servant church responds to individuals, whoever they are and whatever they need. As the Leet Memorial Church illustrates, Servants know people by name and reach out to help them one by one. In a small town like Bradford, Illinois, this is a way of life. Yet whatever the context—rural, urban, or suburban—Servants share Leet's moderate and accepting faith, and its steady commitment to share its neighbors' burdens.

BRADFORD, ILLINOIS

If you're in Tiskilwa and you want to get to Bradford, don't bother to ask for the county road by number. "What? Boy, I sure don't know." Just ask for the place. "Bradford? Oh, that's easy!" And if you pay attention as you drive through the low, quiet hills, and you watch the landmarks along the way, in about twenty minutes you'll catch the main road at the Boyd's Grove church. Turn right, and it will take you straight into Bradford. It wouldn't have helped to know the numbers of the roads—none of them are marked anyway. People in this part of Illinois don't need that. They know the land and the roads, and the towns, and the people.

The road into Bradford from the east cuts straight across rich, black fields carpeted with stubble from the corn harvest. When you cross the single railroad track you'll pass Shallowbrook Farm, its white fences, red buildings, and green grass spreading along the road. Then the houses become more frequent—some large Victorians on wide lawns, some more modest homes. As you approach the only stop sign in Bradford, on your right is the Leet Memorial United Methodist Church—a solid red brick building, attractive in its simplicity.

Straight ahead, the business district of Bradford is two blocks long. There is a Red Fox food store and a Rexall Pharmacy, Spinner's Restaurant and Lounge, Foster Electric, Casey's General Store and gas station, four taverns, and several other businesses.

But the auto parts store is closed now, and so is the cafe. The laundromat looks deserted, though it is still in operation. Several other buildings along Main Street are empty. The gas station around the corner is out of business. Bradford is not thriving; in fact, the pattern has been clear for thirty or forty years. In the middle of one block, however, is the Bradford Senior Citizens Center, and a sign out front proclaims, "We're Not in Our...," with a picture of a rocking chair.

Behind Main Street are several blocks of modest old frame houses on large lots that run together. The streets are paths of aging pavement, with no curbs and occasional patches of sidewalk. Houses are cheap in Bradford—cheap to buy, cheap to rent. Even the larger homes cost less than half what they would in Peoria, thirty-two miles away.

Affordable housing draws some newcomers to Bradford. Others simply want to leave the city of Peoria and enroll their children in a small-town school system. Some of the newcomers have quickly become involved in the town, even on the town board. A good portion of them come to Leet Church.

LEET MEMORIAL UMC

The church has been there since 1875, and descendants of its founders still worship there. (The country church at Boyd's Grove, with which Leet is yoked, was founded even earlier, in 1851.) The sign out front is simple: LEET MEMORIAL UNITED METHODIST CHURCH. 9:15 SUNDAY SCHOOL, 10:30 WORSHIP SERVICE. WORSHIP HIS MAJESTY. And at the bottom, in matching simplicity, PASTOR BOB BALDWIN. The entrance is back from the road along the driveway, beneath twin brick pillars that lift a single bell.

Leet Church is growing right now. Church leaders can name young adults who grew up in Bradford families and have returned to the town during the past few years. They have "a strong feeling about their roots," say the elders. Others who have been on the church rolls throughout the years are becoming more active now as they have children of their own. Kids in the church talk with their friends at school, and the friends begin coming to church. Adult members speak enthusiastically of "the reemergence of MYF activities" (Methodist Youth Fellowship).

ACCEPTANCE AND CARING

But it's not only youth—adults are coming to the church as well. New and returning members feel accepted here. Some of the leaders speak of "the catholicity of the Methodist Church": they accept everyone. Newcomers feel as if they fit. There are some limitations to this, though, that trouble the pastor. The church tries to reach out to all kinds of people, he says, because this is what Christ would have them do. Yet the poorer people in town do not attend Leet Church, or its neighboring churches either. Rather, they drive twenty miles to a Pentecostal church, or to the Assembly of God. Pastor Bob is disappointed, recalling John Wesley's insistence that "we reach the poor and bring them into the house of God." For him, even though these low-income neighbors are in another church, the Leet congregation is missing an important element of its historic call to ministry.

But for townspeople who feel enough like their neighbors to worship together, the openness of Leet Memorial is attractive. "They let you think for yourself," says one longtime member. "They don't tell you what to believe." According to Pastor Bob, they "encourage people to work out their own salvation." Because the congregation as a whole is moderate in its theology—not extremely conservative or liberal—it is able to incorporate members at each end of that spectrum, with acceptance for all. More than anything, say the members, the church preaches the love of God. For some who were brought up on "judgment, hellfire, damnation, and fear," this is a welcome message indeed.

But the most persistent and pervasive key to this congregation is found in what they feel they do best: "Whenever there is a need, the church is there," they say. Members tell stories, naming people whom everyone knows. When Eleanor had cancer, people called and came to see her before and after her surgery. They brought meals for Velma's family when her husband died. "They're good at food here," says Don, one of the current leaders. "I don't care if it's appendicitis, a new baby, or an auto accident—they act as if it were due to malnutrition!" Simple, practical care is their specialty.

It doesn't matter if the person in need is a member of the church or not—they care for all. Don tells how he and his wife took in a woman and two children who were stranded in a blizzard while traveling near Bradford. "It makes you feel real good," he says simply, as though he had been granted a privilege he didn't deserve.

Beyond Leet Church, mutual support is a community personality, a way of life shaped by years of pitching in to help each other. Bradford is a farming town, and the farmers are people of independent, self-reliant spirit. Through the years, when one had an accident or became ill, his neighbors did not make a big deal of it; simply, matter-of-factly, they brought in the machinery and worked the fields. No fuss, no intrusion, no obligation—just practical help that met their needs while honoring their independence.

Many of the people in Bradford have known each other for generations. They have watched kids grow up and have their own kids. They know who is in need. And among the church members, most will respond. Often a handful of people take the first step to organize a response, then ask for help throughout the church; and the majority are willing. Some younger women work, which limits their availability. And some older members cannot do much now, but they were active for years, and people remember it. This is a church full of stories. Both the receiving and the giving bind the congregation together.

CONGREGATIONAL LIFE AND COMMUNITY OUTREACH

Leet Memorial United Methodist has 258 members; eighty to 120 attend on an average Sunday, including a number who come but do not belong. In fact, about twenty nonmembers give regularly to the church. Worship is important to this congregation; they love to sing, and they love traditional hymns and choruses. When the organist wanted to add a trompette stop to the old organ, the church readily gave $7,500 to do it. It makes a difference in the sound and the singing, they say.

The youth group, which incorporates twelve-to-nineteen-year-olds, mixes fun, devotional programs, and service projects. Not long ago, for example, they held a food drive in the form of a scavenger hunt, going to homes of people in the church and in the community. Parents have become involved in the youth program, and the whole church feels the kids' presence. An adopt-a-grandparent program offered kids the opportunity to choose older members of the church for special attention. Some of these intergenerational pairs became quite close, and now, several years later, church leaders smile as they talk about one boy who still sits with his "adopted grandmother" in church every Sunday. In a town as small as Bradford it is often difficult for teenagers to find focus and purpose; the adults are concerned to keep the kids in the town—and in the church.

The Sunday school is strong, including three adult classes. The United Methodist Women's group is active. It has been through a transition, say church leaders, because so many women are working now. But it has done a good job of reshaping its schedule and sustaining its commitment.

When leaders of the Leet congregation are asked about their community outreach, they answer with stories about their responses to particular people in need. In fact, they are known for this in the town. Don recalls with a quiet pride how a man in the community said that if he were to go to any church, he would attend Leet because there he saw people helping other people.

In addition to the many individual works of mercy, over the years the church has institutionalized its caring in more organized programs. It sponsors a food pantry and distributes Christmas baskets for the community. The church is a center for the Red Cross and the Salvation Army, and the pastor administers the local Salvation Army fund. A number of members are involved in the town on their own—in the rescue squad and other community services. "We balance faith and works pretty well, I think," says one member. "Well, we try," responds another.

CHURCH AND COMMUNITY PROJECT

Into this congregation of quiet, faithful caring came the invitation to develop a new community ministry program, and the offer of resources to seed it. The core committee members assigned to recommend a project did all the right homework in studying their community. They reviewed census data and ten-year projections; they interviewed residents; they plotted the economic and social profile of the town and the surrounding county.

But the real key to focusing their project came one day when Henrietta and several of her friends got in a car and drove around the town. Henrietta is a fourth-generation member of Leet Church, active both in the church's helping ministries and in the town's senior citizens organization. She and two or three other seniors rode up and down the streets of Bradford that day, spotting where all the elderly in town lived. They knew them all by name, and they came back with a list of all the older residents, which ones were widowed or ill or dependent, and where each one lived. The committee knew from their research that 50 percent of the townspeople were over the age of fifty, but it took Henrietta's human inventory to bring the need to life for them.

And so, putting the needs of these seniors together with their concern for the youth of the town, they designed a program in which they train teenagers to do yard work and home maintenance for senior citizens who can no longer care for their property themselves. The kids work in crews, supervised by adult volunteers; elderly residents pay to hire them if they can afford it, but are not turned down if they cannot pay. The familiar red T-shirts with an outstretched hand and a phone number to call are recognized all over town, and the young workers wear them proudly.

Through this program seniors receive help to remain independent at home as long as possible, and teens receive job-skills training and a modest wage. In addition, program leaders have found that both groups benefit from the relationships that form between them. The seniors request favorite workers, and often provide soda pop and snacks for them. The teens spend time talking and listening to the elders.

The kids' work has become known throughout the community, and they are proud of what they are doing. Church leaders talk about the growth they have seen in the young people, and they name kids who have made, in their words, "a 180-degree turnaround." They speak of one boy, for example, who has changed "from a shy follower to a developed leader," and they say, "We like to feel we were a major part of that." The seniors, for their part, benefit from both the work and the relationships. "I always enjoy visiting with them," says one woman, with a quiet smile.

A New Shoe That Fits Like an Old One

Church leaders describe this ministry program as a new adventure for the church, but one that is consistent with members' faith. "Though it's a new shoe," says one, "it fits pretty good." It grows naturally out of their pattern of responding to persons in need—both the elderly and the young people. They also point out that it fits their Methodist heritage "clear back to Wesley," adding in matter-of-fact terms, "The way he got after his job is pretty well the way we get after ours."

The ministry is new for them in some ways too. Building a program that operates outside the church has been a new experience. Partnership came naturally to this congregation, but the structures for decision making were new. The church had already developed a particularly strong bond with St. John the Baptist Catholic Church. When the Leet church burned in the 1930s, St. John's offered its hall for a fund-raising dinner. Later, when the St. John's hall needed repair, Leet offered its building. The two churches began forming a bridge in the community—a bridge that was strengthened when the parochial school closed, bringing all the children in the town together. That drew the whole town closer, and these two churches in particular have worked in partnership ever since. They help each other when members are in need, and the two women's groups still hold dinners together.

So St. John's was a natural partner in the new project. St. Timothy's Lutheran Church joined as well, and the First Baptist Church sent a representative to the board for several years. Together the partners tackled the job of developing a board of directors that would represent the churches and the community at large. The Leet church is represented but does not control the organization, and some Leet members were confused and disappointed when the board took a shape that limited their participation. Church leaders say it has required a good deal of commitment, not only to start a major new program like this, but to sustain the church's support as the ownership of the project moved out of the church and into the community.

But they have done it. And when Pastor Bob talks warmly of the current sense of renewal in the church—a "rekindling time," in his words—he insists that the Church and Community project has played a big part in it. The renewal is apparent in the new vigor of the church's youth program and in the increased church participation by some adult members. Don himself is a good example. He was only marginally involved in the church when Pastor Bob "shanghaied" him (as Don gently kids his pastor) into chairing the core committee. His investment in this program rekindled his commitment to the congregation as a whole; since then he has become increasingly active, including teaching an adult Sunday school class.

And the congregation wants its own sense of new vitality to "splash over into the community" (in the pastor's words). Their community ministry project has given them a channel through which that can happen, for it has deepened their ties with the other churches and broadened their reach into the community. And in each teenager who changes before their eyes, in every senior citizen whose lawn is cut and whose heart is warmed, their faith spreads. "We think it's going to happen!" says Pastor Bob. And it is happening—one neighbor at a time.

SERVANT CHURCH: THE SHAPE OF MINISTRY

Like many churches, Leet Memorial United Methodist shows signs of more than one image. While there is some Pillar character to the congregation, for example, the predominant Servant image is evident in a number of ways.

Moderate Individualists

Servant churches are generally moderate in their theology and conservative in their social attitudes.[1] Members of the Leet congregation talk about "the catholicity of the Methodist Church." Their open acceptance of different views reflects the moderate character of their shared faith. Because they are not committed to extremes in doctrine, cause, or program, Servants can incorporate members across the theological spectrum.

For the Leet congregation, and for many Servants, this acceptance of people with different beliefs is deeply rooted in their experience of the love of God. Members tell how important this emphasis is in the life and worship of the congregation. There is no hellfire and damnation at Leet—only the gospel of love.

Servant members tend to be more like each other in their social views than in their theologies, owing perhaps in part to their typical similarity in social circumstances. The members of Leet are generally alike in such characteristics as economic standing, education, and occupational level. For the most part they have the same stake in their community, and they see social and political issues in similar ways. As Pastor Bob found to his sadness, the people in Bradford who live at a lower economic level—and therefore might see social issues differently—do not feel comfortable in Leet or any of the town churches.

The Servant church's acceptance of a variety of people also arises from a deep-seated individualism. At Leet, members and pastor alike emphasize that the church does not tell anyone what to believe. They think for themselves; they work out their own salvation. They do not intrude on each other's souls.

While this respect for the individual makes room for people with differing beliefs, it also tends to limit the sense of intimacy within the congregation. Servant churches typically have lower feelings of group cohesion than all the other four images.[2] This does not mean that the members dislike each other. Far from it—they like and respect each other and enjoy worshiping together, just as most other churches do. But, in general, members of Servant churches feel less directly involved in the congregation's decision-making processes, and they tend to spend less time with their fellow members socially, outside of church activities.

In short, Servant churches gather as individuals, even as they minister to individuals. In a rural town like Bradford, the self-reliant ethos of the farmers clearly contributes to this pattern. The town's life-style has been shaped by generations of farm families who lived parallel and cooperative lives, but remained fundamentally independent.

And many Servant churches are located in rural areas or small cities. Not all are rural, however. There are strong Servant congregations in cities and in suburbs; they share the Servant's characteristic individualism and moderation, lived out in their own styles according to their own circumstances. The gospel of love finds its natural extension in ministries of compassion to their neighbors, whatever their needs.

Ministries of Care for Persons

True to their moderate nature, Servant churches are not often inclined to launch fiery crusades or comprehensive programs. Servants simply want to help people, one by one, and their social ministries tend to focus on the needs of individuals. Leet Church's history of outreach is built on ready responses to persons in crisis: "Whenever there is a need, the church is there." All their stories are told by name; every person receives attention as needed.

Characteristically, Leet's Church and Community ministry project was shaped by listing the senior citizens in town who were in need. Henrietta's head count was not just an expression of small-town familiarity—it was true to the Servant's concern for individuals, whatever the context. The planning committee had the same information from census data, but personalizing the issue with neighbors' names and faces moved them to act. Servant church leaders can mobilize great resources of human compassion when they appeal to their congregations with the real needs of people around them.

Perpetual Care

While Servant churches reach out to meet a wide variety of human needs, a number of them design ministries that sustain people through long-term needs. Leet's concern for senior citizens is characteristic of Servant congregations. As compared with the Pilgrim's quest for improvement in people's opportunities in American society, the Servant often takes up the yoke of service when there is little hope of improvement in a person's fundamental condition. In the face of such circumstances, the Servant steps in to ease the burden by sharing the load in whatever ways it can. For Leet, that includes providing help with the continuing needs of home maintenance for seniors who can no longer manage such work on their own.

The Christian Service Program in Canton, Illinois, is another good example of a Servant ministry. The First Congregational United Church of Christ, a Servant congregation, joined together with St. Mary's Catholic Church to help senior citizens with Medicare and insurance forms. While that may seem a modest goal on the surface, CSP lightens the financial and stressful burden for a number of its neighbors who face health crises in their later years.

The distinctive way in which Servants go about their ministries becomes clearer when we compare the Canton and Bradford programs with a ministry for senior citizens that was developed by a Pillar church in the town of Morton, Illinois, just an hour away from Canton. The Community United Church of Christ in Morton also had a concern for senior citizens, but, characteristic of a Pillar, it identified a broad issue and created a professional program to address it. The community research data told the members that there were growing numbers of homebound frail elderly, cared for by family members. In response, Community UCC and eight partners developed a day care center for seniors, providing social stimulation and health monitoring for the participants and relief for their caregivers.

The Servants and the Pillar all engaged in significant ministry to the same target group—senior citizens. But they did it each in their characteristic style. To the Pillar the seniors were a community issue, to be addressed with a comprehensive program. To the Servants, as in Bradford, they were neighbors with names and faces, to be helped through one-on-one ministry. Pastors and other leaders who recognize the church's self-image can help to create ministries that express the congregation's concerns and commitments in ways that make good use of their distinctive gifts.

Reaching People, Not Systems

In their characteristic focus on individual neighbors in need, Servants tend to see people rather than systems. Although they may be aware of justice concerns in broad terms, they do not often analyze social evils in structural terms.

At times, however, Servants speak out when they come to see dysfunction in social systems through their experiences with individuals in need. The Christian Service Program in Canton, for example, learned firsthand through direct service how much trouble their elderly neighbors had in reading and completing Medicare forms; in response, they began to urge governmental authorities to simplify the forms.

The board in Bradford occasionally discussed questions about broader structural problems, but they never saw justice issues that were compelling enough to take a public stand. Their ministry was to particular neighbors in need. Servant church leaders may want to stretch the members' faith by raising broader issues as they emerge from the church's experience with individuals. They should do so patiently, however, remembering that Servants most naturally respond to people; advocacy for systemic justice is unfamiliar territory for most.

A Few Neighborly Partnerships

In general, Servant churches form only a few partnerships, and they turn more often to other churches than to agencies. When Leet Church began planning its Church and Community ministry, it turned to its longtime partner, St. John the Baptist, and two other churches in town. The three partner churches all knew and cared for the townspeople in the same way as Leet did. As the farmers had always joined together to help a sick neighbor, so the churches pitched in to help the town's elderly.

In Canton, the First Congregational UCC Church was right across the street from St. Mary's. Although the two churches had not formally cooperated on ministry projects before, they had a sense of shared turf, and many of their members were neighbors who had known each other for years. The partnership itself proved to be one of the most rewarding experiences for program leaders from both congregations. Servants who do form partnerships can gain resources for their ministries of help—and can make friends in the process.

The Pastor as Shepherd

Servant churches look for leaders who are, above all, caring shepherds of the flock. The Leet congregation displays its relationship with its minister on the signboard out front: he is "Pastor Bob Baldwin." A Pillar church, by comparison, would have written "Rev. Robert Baldwin," to demonstrate its professional respect. What matters most to the Servant, however, is pastoral care. Whether sermons are impeccably crafted or the minister runs a tight administrative ship is less important. Most of the Leet congregation look to Bob primarily as a caregiver, and he is comfortable with that role. In return, the members care for the pastor and his family with the same steady, practical love they show to each other.

Pastor Bob quietly cares for his people without intruding on their independence. For example, since he came three years ago he has "encouraged them to be in the word of God." Compare his approach with that of Rick Sutter, at the Survivor church in South Chicago, who wants to "tie 'em up and feed 'em." Both seek to draw their members deeper into the scriptures; but the needs and style of Servants are different from those of Survivors, and these two pastors are wise enough to understand and respond appropriately. Rick takes an aggressive approach to binding up the wounds of people who are weary from their crises; Bob quietly encourages his independent parishioners to enrich their own faith lives.

Pastor Bob has told his congregation, "I'll preach, marry, bury, call, and win people for Christ. You people run the church."

When asked if the congregation looks to their pastor to equip them for their ministries of help, Bob smiles and shakes his head. "They would do all this stuff anyway," he says, "even if I weren't here." He thinks it over for a moment and then adds, "But they like encouragement. They like to hear from the gospel that this is what Jesus did, or would do, and that this is what the church in Acts did."

And in his simple encouragement, setting their actions in gospel context, Bob Baldwin helps his people to appropriate their ministry experiences into their own lives. Servant people—in fact, members of all styles of churches—become changed in quiet but significant ways by their own acts of mission, as their pastor names the meaning for them.[3]

The Negative Image

The very gift of the Servant church—its tireless care for individuals in need—sometimes leads more to weakness than to strength. When they do too much, Servants can create or prolong dependency in the people they seek to help. Because their own call to serve is so strong, and the experience of helping someone in need is so satisfying to their Christian values, Servants sometimes have a difficult time knowing when to let go—to push a neighbor to stand on his or her own. Leaders of Servant churches need to be aware of this danger and guide the congregation to find ways of building the self-sufficiency of the people they seek to help.

BUILDING ON SERVANT CHURCH STRENGTHS

Most churches claim an element of the Servant in their identity. The biblical mandates to feed the hungry, clothe the naked, and care for the sick are just too strong to be overlooked in congregations' motivations for ministry. And most of us can tell our own stories of times when we were cared for by Servant people.

Servant congregations bring a quiet steadiness to the wider ecology of churches. Moderate in faith and ambition, they are less swayed by trends that sweep across the landscape than are other churches.[4] They are not interested in rocking the boat of society by fiery crusades, nor are they threatened in their own viability. Simply, quietly, they go about doing whatever needs to be done for their neighbors. They are the givers of perpetual care, without whom the other, more eye-catching images could not long stand.

7 Leadership in Claiming and Using Images

FINDING SELF-IMAGES

There is no simple index to congregational values and commitments, no numerical scoring of shared experience. Pastors, lay leaders, and others who care about congregations will not find in this book a grid for pinpointing a church's character. Rather, self-images live and breathe in the congregation's stories, symbols, and life-style. Simply by reading this far, each reader probably has developed an opinion about the images represented in his or her congregation—as that person sees it. But beware of relying on one opinion only. If an image is to be helpful in shaping the church's life and work, it must be recognized and affirmed by the congregation, or at least by the key leadership group.

In this chapter we reflect on how images are recognized and various images interact, the pastor's role in helping the congregation to identify and build on its images, and the potential for bringing about change in congregations through selectively emphasizing particular self-images.

Recent work in congregational studies has given us guidance for understanding the identity of a congregation.[1] Such elements as history and heritage, symbols and rituals, language, saints, and stories all give access to the congregation's deep-seated sense of itself. One face of that multidimensional portrait is its self-image in community ministry.

Guided by the frameworks and methods offered by scholars, tested by years of leading and loving the congregation, pastors and other leaders can not only listen to what the members say but hunt for clues to what members assume without saying. What language do they use in talking about their church, their neighborhood, their faith experience? What formal or informal symbols mark their life together? What kinds of stories do they tell? How do they reach out to their community and—even more important—how do they explain why they do it?

In order to create wider ownership of the images, church leaders can hold group discussions to draw out members' views and experiences. The simplest way is to present the five images in brief summary form, then invite the group to respond. But merely identifying an image is not enough. Why does that image seem to fit the congregation? How do members see it lived out in church programs or goals? When did it begin to appear in the life story of the church? What subgroups within the congregation hold differing images, and how do those images interact in the whole dynamic of church life?

Another method for helping the congregation and its leaders to identify the church's self-image is making a time line of the church's history.[2] As the group shares in charting the events, crises, and leaders that live in congregational stories, the moderator can ask what those landmarks mean to them. The identity of a congregation is found less in its history than in its shared memory—not just what they did, according to an "objective" record, but what it meant to them at the time and means to them today.

The most significant insights come, for example, not in knowing who pastored the church during which years, but in how a previous pastor is remembered and what characterized the church under that person's leadership. Similarly, the question is not the dates of crises in the church's history—a fire, a family tragedy, an unexpected gift—but how the congregation responded to those crises.

As the flow of the church's story takes shape on paper around the walls of the meeting room, reflective leaders will find clues to the congregation's self-image. It will not be said by name, but patterns of language, emphasis, and interpretation will all point toward the distinctive character of the church.

RECOGNIZING HOW IMAGES INTERACT

Rarely is there a single controlling image for a congregation. As members, leaders, and circumstances shift through the years, images modulate like melodies moving through major and minor variations. At any given time, different groups or individuals will see the church differently. The pastor may hold one image and the board or council another; active leaders may see things differently from pew warmers; judicatory staff may hold an interpretation that is at odds with that of the local group. Recognizing the contrapuntal twinings of two or three images can help leaders to understand congregational behavior.

A pastor in Denver, for example, found a key to persistent disagreements in his congregation: "No wonder this church fights so much," he said. "We used to be a Pillar, but we're not anymore. We're a Survivor now. There's a group in the church that still thinks we're a Pillar, and there's a group of more recent members that knows we're a Survivor. No wonder they can't agree on what we should do!"

When congregational leaders begin to recognize how members hold differing images of the church, they can find appropriate ways to build support for ministry. To begin with, leaders can emphasize the broader vision of the church and its mission that all the members share. That core of shared faith and mutual commitment to the church provides the secure foundation that allows members to differ in their views and their styles of doing ministry.

Building on that base, then, leaders can emphasize different perspectives and even use different language when presenting ministries to subgroups within the congregation. For example, if the social concerns committee wants to expand the church's involvement in health ministries, in talking with a Prophet subgroup they may emphasize the dysfunction in the national health-care delivery system; with Servants, on the other hand, they may tell stories of persons in their church or neighborhood who have suffered from inadequate care.

In this way church leaders can use their analysis of images and subgroups to gain broad support for new ministries, and to develop an ecology of ministry within the congregation, making the most of members' characteristic orientations and gifts. While individuals act from a variety of motivations and styles, often Servants are ready to give hands-on care, Prophets to carry the banner of justice, and Pillars to connect the church with communitywide efforts. Pilgrims understand the importance of culture and hard work, and Survivors come through in an emergency. Pastors and other leaders who watch for these patterns can encourage members in roles that use their gifts well and satisfy their distinctive calls to ministry.

EXPECTATIONS OF PASTORAL LEADERSHIP

Each congregational image looks for particular qualities in its pastors. These may be articulated at times of pastoral change or may lurk beneath the surface as unstated expectations. Whatever their expression, they are often a key to a congregation's sense of satisfaction or dissatisfaction with its pastor, precisely because they reflect how the congregation sees itself. These profiles are never simple—all churches want their pastors to care for the members, for example, and to preach inspiring sermons. Yet they do highlight some of the strongest values in different styles of congregations.

The Pillar church, above all, seeks professional quality leadership from clergy and laity alike. As at West Street Church, quality is important in everything Pillars do—from worship and preaching to music to Christian education to building maintenance. Many Pillars are relatively large churches, often with a number of business and professional persons among the members. They want a highly competent professional at the head of the organization.

For the Pilgrim, tradition is the key. This congregation looks for a pastor who celebrates and represents the heritage at its best. Often this includes sharing an ethnic identity with the congregation, but not always—and ethnic commonality alone is not enough. What is more important is that, like Charles McGowan, the pastor knows and honors the cultural-faith tradition. The Pilgrim pastor who understands the congregation's sense of its tradition, and who coaxes the church to live up to the best of that tradition and move beyond it, can be both beloved and effective.

The Survivor church needs a pastor with the strength and tenacity to keep going when things get tough. Because of their own constant struggles, Survivors often place intense demands on the minister. As at South Chicago Church, many of the members face personal crises, and the church itself lives at the borders of viability. The pastor needs reserves of strength to summon for meeting midnight traumas and chronic budget crises—and must also be wise enough to protect his or her personal life from being devoured by the needs of the church.

Prophets look for an energetic visionary to lead them in new quests. Some Prophets, like Shalom, know their own social agenda and seek a pastor who will join them on the front lines. Others, like Edwin Ray, will risk following their pastor into new areas out of their love and trust for her or him. Whether Prophets by passion or by permission, these congregations are ready to give their loyalty and restless energy to the person with the charism.

Servant congregations look for, above all, a good pastor to shepherd the sheep. As at Leet Memorial Church, Servant members will go on about their caretaking without instruction, but they love to hear their pastor say that this is the way Jesus would have them live. That attentiveness to encouraging them in their work, coupled with a quiet, unobtrusive style of individual caring, will nourish them in their lives of service.

Stated baldly as they are here, these roles may seem intimidating. But the point is *not* that every pastor must perfectly fulfill these types. Rather, these descriptive sketches can serve as frameworks for emphasis in ministry. Pastors who have struggled with expectations that they be all things to all people can take comfort in identifying the roles that mean the most to their particular congregation. And in times of crisis or transition, a pastor can help stabilize and reassure the congregation by giving special care to those key aspects of his or her ministry.

For these characteristics represent what different congregations most appreciate and admire in their leaders. Not only do the members look for these elements in their pastor, but they find them. They respond instinctively to any positive expressions of these roles, and in doing so they can encourage and help to define the pastor's own gifts.

THE PASTOR'S ROLE IN CLAIMING CONGREGATIONAL IMAGES

By nature and by definition, self-images emerge from the congregation: from the church's remembered and continuing story; from the members' values, commitments, and life experiences. Any symbol holds power because it points to something beyond itself. The images described in this book have no generative power in and of themselves; they cannot be chosen at will by any one leader and put on like a new suit of clothes. Rather, they can be instruments of renewal to the extent that they express who the congregation sees itself to be—and who it wishes to become.

But because members hold differing and fractional views, the pastor plays a key role in identifying the operative images of the church. The pastor cannot create the church's identity, but he or she often names it and calls it forth. This means that the pastor must first of all listen to the congregation—listen to the spoken and the unspoken, the stories and the symbols, the groups and the individuals. The pastor not only watches what the congregation does, but tries to understand *why* they do it. And he or she looks for the ways in which different images support and compete with each other within the congregation.

But more than this, the pastor has a responsibility to engage the church's story in continuing dialogue with the larger story of the Almighty at work among us, testing the congregation's self-images against the historical and eternal vision of God's realm. The shape of that larger vision is both universal and particular. It is universal in its core content of Christian doctrine, handed down through the ages in scripture and tradition. But it is also particular as it is appropriated and interpreted by each congregation.

Part of the pastor's job, then, is to guide the congregation in a process of exploring the nature of its own faith. Engaging the church in studying the scriptures, in reflection, and in prayer, the pastor encourages members to ask what God wants of them—both individually and corporately—and helps them to articulate the vision that emerges from that search. This dialogue between the pastor's vision and the congregation's begins in the pastoral search process and continues throughout their life together.

Out of that active reflection, then, the pastor lifts up the images that represent the congregation at its best and most faithful, according to the church's own sense of God's call as well as the pastor's convictions. Naming that identity for the church, he or she then leads the congregation in nourishing and exercising those positive images, and neglecting—or challenging, when necessary—any negative ones.

On some occasions a pastor may need to name the vision aloud and challenge the congregation with its implications. Especially at times of crisis or celebration, or when facing watershed decisions, the congregation may need to be called by name, as Samuel was called.

More often, the pastor leads through quieter means to help the congregation claim its identity. Sermons, prayers, and the style of worship not only express the character of the congregation, but also help to shape it. On boards and committees the pastor, working together with lay leaders, can midwife decisions and programs that honor what is best in the congregation's self-image and stretch beyond it. Where the pastor has influence on appointments to key boards and committees, his or her strategic deployment of the members helps to define the shape of the program or process that will emerge.

Through these and countless other subtle and supportive means, a pastor guides a congregation in living out what is best in its self-images. The images must dwell within the heart of the congregation, and the members will confirm or deny them by their responses. The more the exploration and the guidance are shared with the lay leadership team, the stronger the process will be. And through it all, over the years, the congregation helps to shape the pastor, even as the pastor helps to call forth the nature of the congregation.

To root church leadership in the congregation's self-image, then, means neither quiescence nor manipulation. It is not as passive as saying, in effect, "Whatever is, is right," nor as aggressive as creating a new identity from outside the church's experience. Rather, the pastor exegetes the congregation—drawing out the meanings represented by different segments of the church, analyzing those messages in the context of the gospel story, and leading the congregation to offer its best response to God's call.

IMAGES AND CONGREGATIONAL CHANGE

Naming is not a passive act. To name is not only to acknowledge identity; it is to summon and even to shape it. The ancients believed there was power in names, especially the names of kings and gods. In our own times, gospel hymns sing of the name of Jesus. New parents choose names that represent what they hope their children will become. Nicknames and epithets shape our self-consciousness.

In the same manner, congregational self-images not only reflect our identity as a church, but also help form it. Our images provide a familiar context that enables us to become better than we are. Or, to say it differently, change is rooted in continuity. A congregation can more easily support a new direction in ministry if they can see it as claiming or reasserting something important about who they are and always have been. On the other hand, if they feel they are being asked to become something new and different, they can easily become threatened and discouraged rather than affirmed and energized.

Can a congregation choose to change its self-image? Sometimes—but not beyond the elements that are already represented within it. For example, leaders of a small urban church in Milwaukee decided they were tired of being a Survivor, and they wanted to do something about it. As they looked at the congregation, they felt there was an element of the Prophet within their identity as well. The pastor and key lay leaders decided to emphasize the Prophet in them and neglect the Survivor. "We should live as if it were so," they said. "Then we may become what we live."

Three elements were crucial in this process for them. First, the image they chose to move into already existed within the congregation. Second, the pastor took a leading role in identifying the image and direction, and called for change. And third, the pastor developed the vision together with a core of lay leaders, who recognized it as a positive element of the church's identity and committed themselves to work with the pastor to bring it about.

The pastor who merely acknowledges a congregation's various self-images without examining them in light of the gospel work of Christ, as both pastor and people understand it, may overlook a need or opportunity for growth. But, by the same token, the pastor who imposes a separate agenda on the church takes memory and interpretation out of the congregation's hands—and will probably not have much impact beneath a surface level. At the Milwaukee church mentioned above, the pastor listened to the congregation, called for change through emphasizing the image that she felt represented the congregation at its best, and enlisted significant lay leaders in the vision and the effort. Working together with the congregation as coleaders in the process of their own change, the pastor helped them to begin growing into their chosen self-image.

SUMMARY

Congregational self-images are more than descriptive patterns. They are active, living identities that both reflect and shape our congregations. By listening carefully to the heart and language of the congregation, pastors and other leaders can identify the appropriate images and help the congregation to claim them. Selectively lifting up images that represent the church at its best can enable the members to increasingly grow into them in a variety of ministries of compassion and witness.

8 From Worship to Outreach: Images Focus Congregational Energy

A s we have emphasized throughout this book, the motivational power of congregational self-images lies in recognizing—and celebrating—the unique style of each. Every congregation's life is a slowly shifting kaleidoscope of programs reflecting a variety of deeply held commitments that, taken together, compose the comprehensive unity of its approach to ministry. These patterns reflect not only what the congregation does, but how and why.

Both the Evangelical Covenant Church of South Chicago and Shalom United Church of Christ chose transitional housing for their Church and Community projects, but they approached it differently, each guided by its own self-image. Shalom, the prophetic church, first identified housing issues as important to its members and to their city. In fact, early in its young life the congregation petitioned the national church body to make homelessness a denominational priority. Seeking a local setting to address its issue, it discovered the Lafayette Transitional Housing Center and joined immediately. Within the Center's board of directors, Shalom representatives took a leading role in urging not only the establishment of the Center itself, but also the formation of a citywide task force on affordable housing.

The South Chicago church, by contrast a Survivor church, came to its concern for housing through members' experiences with women they knew personally who had been victimized by domestic abuse. They saw the effects of life-threatening evils on these neighbors—violence, alcohol, drugs, gangs, poverty. And as Survivors, they did what they could to reach out to them: they offered them shelter in a safe place. Through this experience they began to learn more about housing as a broader community issue, and they are sympathetic to the larger goals of the Barnabas Project. But their own energy, stretched thin already by their personal struggles, is poured into helping these particular women in crisis.

AREAS OF CONGREGATIONAL MINISTRY

In the next few pages we look briefly at several areas of congregational ministry, suggesting characteristic styles of each image. These are intended not as comprehensive statements, but as descriptive starting points, to be discussed and fleshed out by interested congregations. In offering these suggestions, we reiterate our warning that only rarely will any congregation fit a profile exactly. Rather than describing their situations, these images may help congregations to see the directions they are moving and to choose the style of ministry, or combination of styles, that they feel most clearly responds to God's call in their circumstances. We will begin with worship at the center of church life and move outward toward strategies for community ministry.

Worship as an Expression of Faith

Worship and spiritual growth are central for every style of congregation. Most churches have basic liturgical elements in common—music and prayer, preaching and sacraments, clergy leadership and symbolic lay participation. Yet in each the worship emphasis is different, shaped and motivated by their congregational self-image.

At West Street Christian, the Pillar church, worship is the hub of members' life together, and they do it so well that it strengthens all the other activities. The congregation takes great satisfaction—and nourishment—from the excellent preaching, fine music, and skilled pastoral leadership. The building carries its accumulated history, yet is modernized to accommodate its current needs. Symbolic of a communitywide concern, Pillar churches put a priority on greeting newcomers and incorporating them into worship.

Worship is equally central to the Immanuel Lutheran congregation, the Pilgrim church. Its relatively formal liturgical style is rooted in its cultural heritage; it provides a bond that not only sustains the members but also draws visitors into the family. The pastor values the congregation's heritage as much as the members do, and celebrates it in their life together. Yet he also encourages them to move beyond it, and leads and supports them in their efforts.

For the Survivor church in South Chicago, where faith is a lifeline, Sunday worship is a welcome gathering of those who have made it through another week. Singing gospel songs and hearing again God's Word read and preached, the members gain strength for the week to come. Recognizing their need, the pastor has concentrated his primary efforts not on pushing for more community involvement, but on building up the body. Small care groups and prayer bonds promise a network of significant nurture and support through the difficult times ahead.

At Shalom United Church of Christ and Edwin Ray United Methodist Church, both Prophet churches, worship is a time of study, spiritual nurture, personal support, and reaffirmation of their commitments to service in the world. In worship they also report on their missional activities during the previous week, and they gather their offerings to support the commitments they have made. With a global consciousness and a local commitment to make an impact, members celebrate what God has given them strength to do, and encourage each other in further work.

The pastor of Leet Memorial United Methodist Church, the Servant church, focuses congregational worship on celebration of the love of God for each member, whatever his or her particular tradition. Members sing their favorite hymns with joy, accompanied by a new stop on the organ. The pastor feels no need to encourage his members to works of mercy; they would help people whether he were there or not, just as they've always done. But, he says simply and reflectively, "They love to hear me say that this is what Jesus would have them do."

Evangelism for Membership

As churches seek to reach out for new members, they provide a window to the values they cherish most and believe will attract others to join them. Churches recruit new members by showing their style where others can see it. In all churches current members bring prospective members, and any style of church may have a committee on evangelism; clear differences appear in what they say and how they approach the task.

For membership growth, the Pillar church depends on its association with the people and programs that hold the community together. The worship sometimes includes longtime prospects, permanent visitors (friends of the church) who enjoy the music, preaching, prayers, and ambiance of worship. Typically the evangelism committee and the pastor both have designated procedures to follow up every name-tagged person with an invitation to church activities, social events, and the regularly scheduled inquirers' class. All the church programs and community activities that use the facilities are potential feeders, but not always directly; often they simply confirm the Pillar's involved civic stance. Special events—from concerts of classical music to public prayers for national crises—remind the community that this church is the crossroads of major concerns.

The Pilgrim church stands at the center of cultural life for the people who call it home. In the old days, Pilgrim churches developed their members biologically—they grew their own. Now the church provides educational evangelism, where youth from many backgrounds can learn the faith as carried by the strength of this congregation's memories. Membership growth happens in traditional events: Church weddings are not only celebrations for the bride and groom, but renewal for the extended family and friends. Funerals provide time, sometimes two or three days, to reknit the networks of family and friends that are scattered by economic necessity. Annual holiday gatherings are accordion events, expanding to attract nostalgic alumni—often far more than the number of sustaining members.

A strong Pilgrim church may shelter and encourage one or more other ethnic congregations under its roof, as Immanuel did with the Chinese and the Eritreans, for they understand the intimate weaving of Christian faith and cultural pilgrimage.

Survivor churches are found by people who discover they need a Christian friend in the difficult but unavoidable transitions of their lives. Loss of a job, death of a spouse, divorce, children in trouble, heavy personal debts—all sorts of pressures help people recognize how vulnerable they are and how much they need one another. Those who have a seat in the lifeboat throw a line to others they find treading water around them; their shared stories of struggle, and the deep faith required to see them through, bind them together.

Survivors are less likely than Pillars to have a committee or an organized program for evangelism. Occasionally they may recognize a member with particular gifts, as the South Chicago church organized the Board of Outreach to bless a young woman's evangelistic gifts. But their strongest outreach comes from members who know how much they have been helped, and who are encouraged to share their stories with others.

Prophet churches get people's attention through community awareness of the issues they pursue. Since these issues are in the public arena, the names of these churches are often found in local newspaper articles and radio interviews. In challenging and seeking to change the status quo, Prophet churches are not reticent to claim their space as they voice their commitments: Shalom uses trademark life-size puppets to dramatize its issues in public demonstrations, and Edwin Ray has more modest signs located in the front yards of the homes it is rehabilitating. Shalom's newspaper ad announces its core commitments to attract potential members: "Inclusive worship, Communion every week, working for justice and peace, global awareness." Prophets need to be aggressive in seeking the people who care about the same issues they do, and who want to act together on their commitments.

Servant churches are typically more laid-back in their efforts to recruit new members, and they tend to attract people who want to help others. They gather people naturally as they are in the act of serving—the patient in the next bed when they visit the hospital, the volunteers who come to help in their soup kitchen. Since they are a gathering of individuals who care about others, they accept as natural that someone might join in their ministries but not in their church membership, even as they accept a diversity of beliefs among their members. The pastor may attract new members through counseling programs, but most Servant evangelism committees concentrate on reclaiming old backsliders. Servants simply keep on helping anyone who needs their help; and if some of those people become part of the church, so much the better. Rather than conducting explicit evangelism programs, both Prophet and Servant churches attract people who want to join in what the church is already doing.

Stewardship of Money

In all congregations members give in gratitude to God and in commitment to purposes that match their sense of congregational vocation. As in worship and evangelism, the self-image of the congregation is often clearly evident in the goals and procedures by which congregations reconfirm members' loyalty in their renewed commitments.

Pillar churches have detailed, carefully constructed budgets to meet. Organized stewardship programs are usually based on annual pledges, given weekly in special envelopes. Members often express a mixture of privilege and obligation in their regular financial support. To match a variety of church and community needs, Pillars raise money for ministry projects through a schedule of special appeals, to which interested members respond. In some Pillar churches the regular income may be supplemented publicly by communitywide annual events, personally by access to major givers in the congregation, and privately by an endowment fund from wealthy families of a former generation.

Pilgrims raise money through loyalty to the family: we have always taken care of our own, and we will continue to do so. Most Pilgrim churches provide stewardship envelopes and encourage financial angels. But sometimes the whole community is incorporated into church support through neighborhood carnivals and nostalgic festivals, often scheduled to celebrate holidays from distant parts of the world. Fund-raising is accompanied by distinctive cooking smells, ethnic delicacies, and a colorful mix of old costumes and casual clothes. In churches that shelter more than one Pilgrim congregation, each maintains a few traditional days and everyone becomes an honorary member of whatever culture is being remembered. Even the calendar in city hall highlights the traditional festivals that rally funding for the Pilgrim church.

The Survivor church, living from one crisis to the next, receives the grateful gifts of members whom the church has sustained in former days. Although members may have little money for themselves, they sacrifice to sustain their congregation and, through the church, to provide a little something for others who seem to need it more than they do. If the church belongs to a denomination, Survivors often receive mission funding from denominational sources and more affluent sister congregations seeking to be helpful. Stories of people in crisis, or those who have been helped through crisis, create strong motivations to give—and Survivors have plenty of such stories.

The Prophet church is the most rigorous in its sacrificial stewardship, helping members to discipline their giving with the same commitment as they focus on social concerns. Like Survivors, they often use stories of crises, but always reaffirmed into a larger cause. Where the Survivor will raise money to help particular persons, the Prophet will tell about individuals in order to illustrate a larger evil to be confronted or a social vision to be achieved. The budget of a Prophet church is lean in spending on itself but hefty in commitments to causes it believes in. Financial resources oscillate between the excitement of its social causes and the valleys of institutional maintenance, as if a neglected church building were a sure sign of its commitment to a greater cause.

The Servant church offers constant opportunities for helping people in need. Most Servant churches have a few members who take special pride in caring for the church building, because, like the Prophet, the rest are so spontaneous in giving to others that they neglect the home base in their altruism. Servants are not highly organized in fund-raising for the church, but they always have a fresh, inviting need to which members can contribute. They often resist large, organized campaigns, but a new opportunity appears each week; some members would be disappointed if it didn't. The Servant simply keeps on helping people as they need it, and Servant leaders keep on asking. Money is always tight, but somehow they always seem to get by.

DEVELOPING STRATEGIES
FOR COMMUNITY MINISTRY

Few congregations have the strength or access to impact their communities alone, but with allies and partners they can make a difference. When united for a common ministry, churches increase their resources, community contacts, and visibility. In concert they make a more public commitment to ministry. But such partnerships do not come easily for most churches. Congregations highly value their independence, and the typical church has little experience in sharing decisions or working closely with others. Congregational self-images provide guidelines for congregational leaders to understand their strengths and weaknesses, their tensions and satisfactions, when they try to work together with others in social ministries.

When they do cooperate, as we note in each case, churches with particular images are attracted toward different styles of partnerships and coalitions. Leaders of Pillar churches may utilize the resources of community agencies and professional services, but they form lasting partnerships with other churches and church groups. Prophet church leaders build coalitions in the opposite direction: they develop relationships with social agencies more often than with churches, and assemble new coalitions of allies for each special campaign.

Congregations of the other images tend to stay closer to their comfort zone, networks they know and feel they can trust. When they work with others, the leaders of Pilgrim churches find partners among their extended cultural or theological family; Servant churches reach for help as the need arises; and Survivor leaders have difficulty establishing partners, but accept help wherever available.

Faced with this array of diverse and somewhat conflicting expectations, partnerships among churches require effort, creativity, and risk. But without venturesome and imaginative combinations, ministries must depend on the limited resources of a single congregation. As the ministries of this book have shown, partnerships that succeed rank among the most productive and satisfying rewards of community ministry.

The key to unity that transcends differences lies in finding common ground. Although churches are inclined to work alone, they overcome their barriers and achieve cooperative strategies when they realize how much they need one another to reach a common goal. The prize must be worth the effort.

Church leaders find a variety of common grounds when they have a genuine commitment to community ministry. Some churches wear different denominational labels but find they have basically the same style in outreach to the community. Churches that share denominational or faith backgrounds often overcome differences in styles of ministry. Churches that recognize a common threat can band together despite years of hostility. But most clearly unified are the congregations that realize a division of labor in a common cause. In all, the basic ingredient is trust.

Partners in Perspective: Similar Self-images

Some combinations of congregations are relatively easy, as if the congregations are drawn together naturally. In the town of Bradford, Illinois, the churches that built their Church and Community ministry had been working together for some time. The Methodist, Catholic, Baptist, and Lutheran pastors—representing theologically different approaches to ministry in the same town—work together naturally to support a program that reaches both youth and elderly. "We always help each other" is their matter-of-fact explanation.

Partnerships based on common perspectives are natural and easy on all participants. They occur in a wide variety of rural towns and urban neighborhoods when congregations see the issues through similar self-image lenses. By mixing several denominational traditions, these partners appear to have crossed many differences. But in their views of ministry, they see and respond to the same world. In these areas of ministry they feel more kinship with their immediate neighbors than with distant denominational connections.

Partners in Faith: Shared Traditions

Some congregations naturally turn for support to the networks of friendship and faith inherent in their denominational families. These partnerships find common ground not in their self-image, but in their shared historical traditions. Marginal Survivor and Pilgrim churches often develop networks through their denominational connections to find Pillar and suburban Servant churches to support their programs with donations and volunteers. Significant faith traditions may cross denominational lines, as when the Church of the Brethren and the Mennonites—different denominations with a common tradition of peace ministries—join in a community ministry of reconciliation.

In Indianapolis, Westminster Presbyterian Church, an urban congregation of eighty members in a depressed community, has developed a mutually helpful ministry with Second Presbyterian Church, a congregation of three thousand members. The city Survivor-Servant provides location and leadership for ministry, while the metropolitan Pillar church finds an outlet for its mission energy through its volunteers and financial support in Westminster's programs of Christian ministry and community care. Each congregation has different gifts to offer and to receive, and both are grateful to find expression within their denominational family.

Edwin Ray Church has the look of a Survivor and the soul of a Prophet. It is small in members, with minimal budget and limited resources; yet it has become the drum major for housing renewal in the community. The United Methodist urban parish that includes Edwin Ray Church embraces unlikely partners. Victory Memorial United Methodist Church is even smaller than Edwin Ray, and every ounce the Servant church. Calvary United Methodist Church, with the largest but most scattered membership, carries its German Evangelical United Brethren heritage in the symbols of its building, the ritual of its worship, and the stories of its members. As a Pilgrim church that has joined the Methodist family, it carries its weight in current ministry while maintaining its distinctive heritage. But (as long as no one mentions "merger") these United Methodist churches—Prophet-Survivor, Servant-Survivor, and Pilgrim—work well together.

Partners in Concern: Threatened Communities

When the community feels threatened, church leaders often rally to overcome historical differences with a united strategy. These sentiments run strong, for example, in endangered rural areas. In one agricultural community that is losing population and is fractured by divisions in the school system, post office, and telephone area code, a strong Presbyterian Pillar church and a determined Lutheran Pilgrim congregation had carried a grudge for eighty years. Members of both churches could name the event, even the year it happened. Throughout the community, members of each church defined themselves by saying clearly how different they were from the other church.

But when the gas station, where they all had gathered and gossiped, abruptly went out of business, families from both churches felt the loss of the last vestige of their community. Amidst that threat, the leaders and members resolved their animosities to save their community. In a demonstration of reconciliation, they publicly joined forces and led the town in building a new community center, with space for a community store where they can continue to gather.

Not every threat is so vivid, nor every reconciliation so dramatic, nor every response so successful. Recognition of a common threat can precipitate a temporary coalition, which in this case has become a lasting partnership. But threat alone will not sustain cooperation. Participating congregations must realize how much more they gain by working together than by working separately.

Partners in Effectiveness: Division of Labor

When the cause is compelling, churches with different images realize how much they gain from a division of labor. Servant and prophetic churches begin at opposite ends of the social justice scale—Servants are inclined to help individuals and Prophets are attracted to challenge dysfunctional systems. Because they are so different, however, when they realize how much each brings that the other needs they often form the best combination to work on a common goal.

When St. Boniface Catholic Church, an urban Franciscan parish with a strong tradition of community care, launched a ministry of transitional housing for homeless people in its community, it documented the need but lacked the resources to meet it. Providentially, it formed an alliance with St. Thomas Aquinas, a Pillar parish near the university, and with Shalom Church, a prototype Prophet with energy and resources restless to be used. The three churches have different histories, memberships, gifts, and theologies. But together they complement each other. United by a shared vision of housing the homeless, their teamwork takes advantage of their differences.

Such a common cause is sometimes strong enough to bridge wide social, cultural, and economic barriers. A sensitive Pillar church may want to work with a Pilgrim or Survivor congregation, but these may be polar opposites in everything from bank accounts to self-confidence. Combined strategies can be developed when each congregation knows the gifts inherent in its image, and honors both the strengths and the limitations of the others.

The Basic Ingredient Is Trust

The backbone of most strategies is common faith and personal trust that develops among the participants. Most community ministries are carried by more formal organizations, but the energy and commitment of participants are nurtured through informal ties. The strongest strategies combine the multiple commitments of common vision, mutual respect, Christian foundations, and vulnerable trust, woven through both the formal organization and the informal network that sustains a ministry.

Thus in the Mustard Seed, for example, the formal structure defines program, sets policies, and pays bills. But the informal structure encourages volunteers, supports the leaders, finds the funding, and even locates the neighbors who need help. The strength of ministry among the partner churches is the combination of formal organization and informal trust. Volunteers who are sensitive to one another can be more tuned in to the people they are trying to reach. As one community leader in Tipton reflected, "The problems hurt more when you know the people by name."

In fact, when the commitments of shared turf and personal trust are strong, precise agreement on a common cause may be less important. In Bradford the participating churches could join freely because they trusted the motives of their partners, even before they knew the details of the program. In the three-church parish of Edwin Ray, trust does not depend on exact agreements but on honoring differences, and on a common commitment to strengthen the community housing and the people who live there. The partners in Lafayette Housing first came together for a common cause, but the long-term success of the project was built on trust among the participants. In strong ministries, the trust at the core has a positive ripple effect far beyond those volunteers who directly participate. At the center, common faith and human trust bind partners together.

CLEAR AND COMPELLING IMAGES

Every church can develop effective community ministries, and grow stronger in the process, when church leaders build on positive congregational self-images. Of many possibilities, we have identified five centering images that describe, predict, and inspire congregations to action. In using these images, leaders release energy and build self-confidence, even in discouraged churches.

These images break through old stereotypes of social and denominational restraints, of liberal and conservative behaviors, of limitations due to size and congregational resources. Through the lenses of these images we see how conservative churches may engage in social ministry, Survivor churches can develop effective programs, and Pillar churches will advocate social transformation.

In the drama of social ministry, congregations often play their roles as if written by script. In service and justice ministries, Prophet churches lead the charge against "oppressive institutions"—a term almost redundant for them, since for Prophets institutions are by nature oppressive. Pillar churches, by contrast, recognize themselves among the leading community institutions; as one pastor observed, "We do social action by telephone—we take care of the problem." Pilgrim churches are ambivalent about justice ministries, joining when their people are involved, but vïgilant to maintain their independent identity. Survivor churches feel alienated, unjustly denied access to the resources of the larger society. Servant churches, busy helping individuals, seem incapable of seeing social structures at all. With minor variations, the script is reenacted in every sort of community.

We have also seen the mixing of images within each congregation and among the community of churches. These images offer a variety of gifts, which each alone can offer to others, and which make them stronger in the act of giving: Pillars can legitimate change, while Pilgrims sustain the strength of history. Survivors can cope where others collapse, and Prophets are never content to leave evil unchallenged. And beyond all the worthy causes, Servants keep a focus on the individuals in need.

Self-images shape congregational choices and styles of leaders, the selection and implementation of program, the cadence of the music, and the content of the prayers. When churches are preoccupied with theologically expected behavior, or with the limitations of church size, or other less compelling forces, these images are often enacted even without being recognized. But when leaders and members are clear, agreed, and committed in their images as the fullest possible expression of God's will for their church, then, by God's grace, previously unimagined ministries seem natural.

Chart:
Churches by Self-Image

Churches by Self-Image

Characteristics of Congregations*	Survivor	Prophet	Pillar	Pilgrim	Servant	N
PARTNERS: Average number of partners per church. Churches, Nonchurch Partners, Total	C .44 N .22 T .67	C 1.33 N 2.67 T 4.00	C 2.00 N .73 T 2.73	C .67 N .50 T 1.17	C 1.50 N .13 T 1.63	(40)
CONGREGATIONAL THEOLOGY: Views on biblical authority and salvation. Evangelical, Moderate, Liberal	E 44% M 44% L 11%	E 33% M 33% L 33%	E 0% M 36% L 64%	E 17% M 67% L 17%	E 0% M 63% L 38%	(40)

Members' Perceptions of Their Congregations**	Survivor 1	Prophet 2	Pillar 3	Pilgrim 4	Servant 5	N	PAIRS SIGNIF. AT P < .01 ***
INTIMACY: Scale measuring social cohesion of congregation. Higher score = greater sense of intimacy	11.5	11.8	11.5	11.7	10.2	(3939)	5 < 1,2,3,4
DECISION MAKING: Scale measuring views of congregational decision-making process. Higher score = more open, participatory process	16.1	15.7	14.9	15.1	14.6	(3076)	1 > 3,4,5 2 > 3,5
ACTIVISM: Individual conscience vs. corporate congregational action on social issues. Scale from 1.0 = individual to 7.0 = corporate	3.9	4.4	3.5	3.7	3.6	(3783)	2 > 1,3,4,5 1 > 3,5

ADVOCACY: Scale measuring priority given to church's advocacy for social justice issues. Higher score = greater priority	10.7	11.0	10.3	11.0	10.6 (3771)	3 < 1,2,4 5 < 2,4
PARTICIPATION: Scale measuring members' participation in social ministry. Higher score = greater participation	4.8	5.4	4.6	5.5	4.0 (2999)	5 < 1,2,3,4 1,3 < 2,4
SOCIAL ATTITUDES: Scale measuring members' orientation to social issues. Higher score = more liberal	13.0	13.5	12.0	14.1	12.1 (3818)	3 < 1,2,4 5 < 1,2,4 1 < 4
GOD OF JUSTICE: Percent agreeing that the church should work for justice	32%	32%	22%	33%	21% (3953)	****

* The first two items consider the 40 churches as the units of analysis, while the remainder are based on individual-level church member data. In the latter, respondents' scores are weighted according to size of church sample, so that each church receives equal weight in the analysis.

** Each of these scales reflects the average response to individual or multiple questionnaire items. Since the number of questions varies, numerical comparison between scales is inappropriate.

*** Test used to determine significance for these items is one-way analysis of variance. Scheffe multiple comparison test used for testing any two pairs of means.

**** Tested using Chi-Square test; significant at < 0.01 level.

Notes

Introduction

1. *Basic Steps Toward Community Ministries,* by Carl S. Dudley (Washington: Alban Institute, 1991), outlines our approach to planning for a congregation-based social ministry program. *Saints and Neighbors: Stories of Church and Community,* ed. Britton W. Johnston and Sally A. Johnson (Chicago: Center for Church and Community Ministries, 5600 S. Woodlawn Ave., 4th floor, Chicago, IL 60637; 1991), records stories told by pastors and lay leaders about their experiences in creating the ministries of the Church and Community Project.

1. Introducing Congregational Self-Images

1. For a survey of images in the New Testament, see Paul Minear, *Images of the Church in the New Testament* (Philadelphia: Westminster Press, 1962).

2. This helpful distinction is developed by Anna Case-Winters in an unpublished paper for a faculty seminar reflecting on the images developed through the Church and Community Project, "Models of the Church: Descriptors, Predictors, and Motivators of Ministry," McCormick Theological Seminary, March 31, 1992.

3. For a brief discussion of biblical and contemporary metaphors and images, and a more extensive list of eight images, see Carl S.

Dudley, "Using Church Images for Commitment, Conflict, and Renewal," in *Congregations: Their Power to Form and Transform*, ed. C. Ellis Nelson (Atlanta: John Knox Press, 1988). We propose the five images in this book based on congregational stories about the intersection between churches and their communities. These were initially discussed by Carl S. Dudley in "Saints, Crises, and Other Memories That Energize the Church," in *Action Information* (Washington, D.C.: Alban Institute, 1989), and by Carl S. Dudley and Sally A. Johnson, "Congregational Self-Images for Social Ministry," in *Carriers of Faith*, ed. Carl S. Dudley, Jackson W. Carroll, and James P. Wind (Louisville: Westminster/John Knox Press, 1991).

4. In its sense of responsibility the Pillar church is similar to "The Congregation as Citizen" in David A. Roozen et al., *Varieties of Religious Presence* (New York: Pilgrim Press, 1984). In its organizational style it resembles "The Church as Institution" in Avery Dulles, *Models of the Church* (New York: Doubleday, 1974). In its social posture it is similar to H. Richard Niebuhr's "Christ Above Culture" in *Christ and Culture* (New York: Harper & Brothers, 1951).

5. In its commitment to cultural continuity the Pilgrim church is similar to the "extended family" of Gaylord Noyce's *Survival and Mission in the City Church* (Philadelphia: Westminster Press, 1975), and in its sense of intimacy it is similar to Dulles's "Mystical Communion," in *Models of the Church*.

6. Although we find no model similar to the Survivor church in relatively recent typologies, in the counterculture mentality of surviving in a hostile world it is often similar to the classic sect described by Max Weber and Ernst Troeltsch (see discussion of countercultural Christianity in Carl S. Dudley and Earle Hilgert's *New Testament Tensions and the Contemporary Church* [Philadelphia: Fortress Press, 1987]) and to Niebuhr's "Christ Against Culture," in *Christ and Culture*.

7. In placing a primary concern on social and political evils of the world, the Prophet church is similar in program to Roozen's "Activist Congregation," in *Varieties of Religious Presence*, and in theology to Niebuhr's "Christ Transforming Culture," in *Christ and Culture*. As a splinter group within a larger congregation it acts more like Noyce's "Revolutionary Cadre," in *Survival and Mission*.

8. In its concern for serving the needs of others, the Servant church is similar to both Dulles's "Church as Servant," in *Models of*

the Church, and Dudley's Servant Church, in *Congregations: Their Power to Form and Transform*.

2. The Pillar Church:
The Story of West Street Christian Church

1. West Street Church membership survey in September 1987.

2. Information from the membership surveys from all the participating churches is compiled in "Churches by Self-Image," the chart on pp. 110–111, which will provide a point of reference for all the chapters of this book. In each reference we note the area of the chart directly concerned in CAPITAL LETTERS, allowing the reader to examine how church members of a particular image responded as compared with responses from congregations with other self-images. In this case we are primarily concerned with the INTIMACY, DECISION MAKING, and PARTICIPATION items.

3. See PARTNERS in the chart, pp. 110–111. N.B.: In comparing church partners we report the average number of church and nonchurch partners, not responses to member surveys.

4. See CONGREGATIONAL THEOLOGY, ACTIVISM, ADVOCACY, SOCIAL ATTITUDES, and GOD OF JUSTICE in the chart, pp. 110–111.

3. The Pilgrim Church:
The Story of Immanuel Lutheran Church

1. See PARTICIPATION and ACTIVISM scales in the "Churches by Self-Image" chart, pp. 110–111.

2. For a discussion of the influence of pastors and other church leaders on volunteers in social ministry programs, see Church and Community Brief Paper No. 7.10, "The Impact on Volunteers Who Participate in Social Ministry Projects," by Sally A. Johnson (Center for Church and Community Ministries, 5600 S. Woodlawn Ave., 4th floor, Chicago, IL 60637; 1992).

3. See SOCIAL ATTITUDES and ADVOCACY scales in the chart, pp. 110–111.

4. See CONGREGATIONAL THEOLOGY profile in the chart, pp. 110–111.

5. From "Lead On, O Cloud of Presence," by Ruth Duck, in

Everflowing Streams: Songs for Worship (New York: Pilgrim Press, 1981).

4. The Survivor Church:
The Story of the Evangelical Covenant Church of South Chicago

1. See CONGREGATIONAL THEOLOGY item in the chart "Churches by Self-Image," pp. 110–111.

2. See SOCIAL ATTITUDES and PARTICIPATION scales in the chart, pp. 110–111.

3. See INTIMACY scale in the chart, pp. 110–111.

4. See ACTIVISM scale in the chart, pp. 110–111.

5. The Prophet Church:
The Stories of Shalom United Church of Christ and Edwin Ray United Methodist Church

1. "The Shalom Vision," Shalom United Church of Christ, Lafayette, Indiana, 1989.

2. See INTIMACY in the chart, "Churches by Self-Image," pp. 110–111.

3. See CONGREGATIONAL THEOLOGY and ACTIVISM in the chart, pp. 110–111.

4. See PARTNERS in the chart, pp. 110–111.

5. See PARTICIPATION in the chart, pp. 110–111.

6. See DECISION MAKING in the chart, pp. 110–111.

7. See CONGREGATIONAL THEOLOGY in the chart, pp. 110–111.

8. See ADVOCACY, SOCIAL ATTITUDES, and GOD OF JUSTICE in the c hart, pp. 110–111.

6. The Servant Church:
The Story of Leet Memorial United Methodist Church

1. See CONGREGATIONAL THEOLOGY profile and SOCIAL ATTITUDES scale in the "Churches by Self-Image" chart, pp. 110–111.

2. See INTIMACY scale in the chart, pp. 110–111.

3. See Church and Community Brief Paper on "The Impact on Volunteers Who Participate in Community Ministries," ch. 3, n. 2.

4. From the results of the Church and Community Planning Inventory, congregational survey taken in September 1987.

7. Leadership in Claiming and Using Images

1. The clearest survey of the elements of congregational identity, along with some of the methods for discovering them, is found in Jackson W. Carroll, Carl S. Dudley, and William McKinney, eds., *Handbook for Congregational Studies* (Nashville: Abingdon Press, 1986). Denham Grierson, in *Transforming a People of God* (Melbourne: The Joint Board of Christian Education of Australia and New Zealand, 1984), focuses on such perspectives as the congregation's sense of time and space, its forms of language and intimacy, and its attitudes toward the past, present, and future. The work of James F. Hopewell in *Congregation: Stories and Structures* (Philadelphia: Fortress Press, 1987), uses literary frameworks of setting, characterization, and plot to trace the congregation's parable story through time.

The Center for Church and Community Ministries has published two papers on congregational identity, both by Carl S. Dudley: "Sources of Congregational Identity," Church and Community Brief Paper No. 2.02 (Chicago: Center for Church and Community Ministries, 5600 S. Woodlawn Ave., 4th floor, Chicago, IL 60637; 1992); and "Congregational Identity as a Basis for Planned Change," Church and Community Brief Paper No. 2.03 (Chicago: Center for Church and Community Ministries, 1992).

2. See discussion on "History," *Handbook for Congregational Studies*, pp. 24–25.